ELVIS
THE GOLDEN ANNIVERSARY TRIBUTE

2

'Music is a beautiful human expression – I love the feeling
I get from it.'

ELVIS PRESLEY 1935–1977

ELVIS
THE GOLDEN ANNIVERSARY TRIBUTE

**Fifty Fabulous Years 1935–1985
in Words and Pictures**

by Richard Peters

**Salem House
Salem, New Hampshire**

By the same author

THE FRANK SINATRA SCRAPBOOK
THE BARRY MANILOW SCRAPBOOK

ACKNOWLEDGEMENTS

For help in researching this book, a special thank you goes to Todd Slaughter and the publishers of *Elvis Monthly*.
All photographs are reproduced by courtesy of the Official Elvis Presley Fan Club of Great Britain PO 4, Leicester, England.

First published in the United States by Salem House, 1985.
A member of the Merrimack Publishers' Circle,
47 Pelham Road, Salem NH 03079.

Library of Congress Catalog Card Number 84-52400

ISBN 0-88162-082-3

Typeset by CCC, printed and bound in Great Britain by William Clowes Limited, Beccles and London

Contents

The Beverly Hills Hotel

For

<u>Elfans Everywhere</u>

'The King' will not be forgotten

Richard Peters

Richard Peters

April 1984

Introduction

'I Remember Elvis'

There is no longer any need for the superlatives. The legend is assured, the fame transcending any changes of fashion or reassessment of history. Elvis Presley was called 'The King' by his admirers while he was alive, and the passage of time since his death has done nothing to diminish his stature. Only the man himself, stripped of the incredible, almost unbelievable trappings of success, remains elusive, an enigma, that million upon million of words of analysis have done little to explain.

Somehow, that is the way it should be for a man who changed the history of modern music and became wealthy and adored beyond any other celebrity this century. For the secret of what makes worldwide success on this scale is an indefinable magic-mix of talent and charisma that is only given to the very few. And Elvis was not only one of the very, *very* few. He was – and remains – unique. In a business in which even the modestly successful is copied and imitated, Elvis resisted every attempt at duplication during his lifetime – and likewise since his death.

Those lucky thousands who actually saw him perform know this to be true. While those others, the uncountable millions, who only heard and loved his music – the very core of his achievement – realise it, too.

The night I first heard Elvis' 'Heartbreak Hotel' there was thunder and lightning in the air; and again, the night his death was announced, a storm was lashing the streets of London. Both events, certainly the second, might almost seem too dramatic to be true, just *too* much of a coincidence. But then Elvis shook up pretty well everybody from the moment he burst on the world of entertainment until the day of his tragic death in 1977, so why shouldn't he be remembered as some kind of elemental force?

Of course, Elvis would not initially have been able to achieve his stunning impact upon our times without the inventive mind of one Thomas Edison of New Jersey who in the year 1877 proudly unveiled his 'talking machine'. His experimentation had produced a piece of equipment which was able to repeat for its astonished listeners the word, 'Hello' and the rhyme 'Mary had a little lamb' which Edison had 'recorded' shortly beforehand. With it he handed the world a means of communication of words and music more immediate and far-reaching than anything before.

There were, of course, artists before Elvis who had used the refinements of Edison's invention to reach their public: but perhaps no one until then had exploited it with such devastating effect. For he created a revolution – and at a time when the world was ripe for change.

In the 1950s a generation of teenagers (of which I was one) were growing up with more freedom, more money and more of a streak of rebellion in them than any previous generation. In particular, they felt a need for values and tastes that were quite different from those of their still war-weary parents.

The first manifestations of this need were on the cinema screen in the films of Marlon Brando and James Dean. From them came new attitudes and new fashions. And then came Elvis with his music and the world was irrevocably changed. His records carried a message (courtesy of Mr Edison) to the far ends of the earth at the greatest possible speed. Their exuberance, their freedom, above all their open, easy sexuality, crystallized what teenagers everywhere felt but could not put into words until Elvis came along.

It was certainly not new for a generation to want to rebel against sexual repression – had not the parents of these self-same teenagers thrown off many of *their* parents' Victorian conventions? But Elvis spearheaded a morals revolution that was more dramatic, more open and undoubtedly more positive than any in the past. He represented a spirit of independence to do and think and act as the individual chose and not as tradition dictated.

The music Elvis sang was also the music he loved – based on the songs of the negro communities close to which he had been born and raised. These tunes, fused with the gospel songs which were another part of his upbringing, and the Country & Western ballads which provided most Southern white folk with their entertainment, became his unique blend of music called Rock 'n' Roll.

It remains to this day a major, though not always recognized, part of Elvis' achievement that he brought the music of the black race to the white. As one music critic wrote a few years back, 'The black sound, or race music as it was then called, was the soul of modern music, but it was mostly ignored by all whites prior to the meteoric rise of a young man with long hair.' Another reviewer added more colourfully, 'Elvis Presley let nigger music out of its cage and rode it, whooping and bucking and ready to boogie all night long, into the secret heart of a generation.'

The respected jazz writer, Peter Clayton, with his profound knowledge of negro music, has perfectly summarised this impact of Elvis on his times. 'Two decades ago,' he wrote in 1977, shortly after Elvis' death, 'any boy with an uncontrollable voice, any girl going through the earthquake of puberty, who at the same time suffered from even slightly restrictive parents, instinctively recognised Elvis as a symbol of escape. His magnificent insolence was an example of how the adult world should be handled. He was freedom, he was sex, he was triumphant youth, for although he was 21 he looked younger. What he stood for could never be

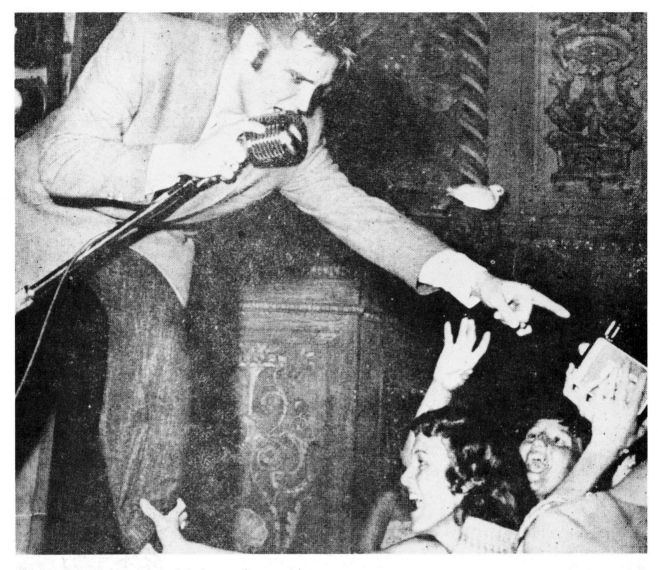

The young Elvis who captured the hearts of a generation.

equated with age, and it was probably at about that time that the ideas of age and death took over from gross sexuality as the obscenities of the era.'

The furore from the older generation which greeted his smouldering, sensual appearance and provocative performances on record or in public was hysterical in tone, and predictably achieved precisely the opposite to its stated intentions. Elvis became even more popular with his fans, eventually passing on the 'mantle' of rebellion to a new generation of musicians, safe in his own ageless talent. Indeed, the excesses of each era since – take the Punks, for example – all owe the climate in which they can express themselves to what Elvis did.

Yet for his part, Elvis never actually had to rebel in his own private life. Naturally polite and courteous, he did not defy his parents, flout the law or authority, or go out of his way to create scandal. And though the accounts of his final years do indicate a certain instability almost certainly brought about by the immense pressures of his fame, he did

not leave a trail of blighted lives behind him as so many superstars have done.

These contradictions may well be another reason why his critics have failed to understand how he, more than any other artist this century, should continue to be the object of such intense interest and admiration years after his death.

Yet the reason is patently obvious. Elvis was much more than a singer with a marvellous voice. He was the personification of a generation: and in particular their adolescence. He was the first intimation of freedom for millions of young people who have now grown to maturity. And that has made him a greater loss than anyone not of that age can realise.

As I said earlier, the enigma of Elvis still remains and I suspect the definitive biography of his life and work may never be written. Elvis himself once said he was going to write his life story, and Colonel Parker, his manager, has hinted from time to time that he has such an undertaking in the works. Elvis, of course, will now never do so, and as for the Colonel? Well, as always, who knows about him . . . ?

In the final analysis, I think it will be seen as Elvis' greatest achievement that he showed the young a new way to live – for pleasure, freedom, sex and the joys of just being *alive*. And his great tragedy was that the fame he achieved quickly excluded him from the element in which his music was most deeply rooted – ordinary human life.

These are just some of the reasons, then, why I remember Elvis, and why I have compiled this tribute to mark the Fiftieth Anniversary of his birth. It brings together not only the facts of his career and the magnitude of his attainments, but also the memories of some of those closest to him in his work as singer and entertainer, surely *the* most important aspect of his life. It is also a way of saying thanks, on my behalf and that of millions of others, for his life. *He will not be forgotten.*

Elvis at the height of his powers – The King of modern music.

The Story of Two Worlds

One Hundred Miles Up Highway 78

In the year 1936 a tornado of awesome power ripped across the town of Tupelo in the heart of the Mississippi bayou country, killing two hundred people and leaving hundreds of others injured and homeless. The town had been nothing much to speak of before – a ramshackle community of mainly wooden houses and small buildings spread across the red-clay soil of the uneven countryside – but the tornado seemed almost like the final straw to the people who grubbed a precarious existence from cotton and the all-but exhausted farmland. As they looked at the devastation all around, these poor white folk, and the even poorer negro families from the outskirts, must have cried for some relief, some sign that God and even the authorities had not altogether abandoned them in this nation still reeling from the effects of the Great Depression.

In truth, the tornado was to be a portent of not one but two significant events in the history of Tupelo. The prayers of the people *were* to be answered and their town rebuilt with an era of prosperity in its wake. And, secondly, a child who survived the terror of that tornado was to shake the nation – and the world – into a new era of musical and social changes that would place the town forever on the map of history. The child was the one-year-old son of a poor sharecropper and his name was Elvis Aaron Presley.

Tupelo, which is located in the northeast corner of Mississippi, not far from the Tennessee state line, could only be described as unprepossessing in the mid-thirties. The thick stands of timber that had once covered the area had long since been cut, and the poor quality soil which remained was gradually eroding into the sluggish, dark-brown bayous. The dense red clay which passed for farm land supported cotton with difficulty and produced weeds more readily than crops.

The climate was humid and oppressive, giving long stretches of unrelenting heat which bred an atmosphere full of stinging insects and made the ground alive with hook worms and snakes. Even the water harboured leeches and typhus. The people themselves – strictly segregated and carefully preserving their racialism – seemed to feel they had missed out on life.

Although the town could boast a Confederate monument near its courthouse, it had not been officially incorporated until well after the Civil War, a state of affairs in the Deep South once described as 'tantamount to being born out of wedlock'.

Despite all this, the people clung to what they had, and Vernon and Gladys Presley, who lived in a small weatherboarded shack (which Vernon and his father had built) beside a dirt-track roadway called Old Saltillo Road, were no different from the rest. Old Saltillo Road was actually located in East Tupelo, the very poorest area of Tupelo separated from the town by a railway, and for this reason many biographies of Elvis Presley have been quick to point out that not only was he born poor but also 'on the wrong side of the tracks'.

Although both Vernon and Gladys were typical Southerners in their speech and manners, Vernon could trace his family tree back to an English immigrant named David Presley (sometimes spelt with a double 's') who had landed in the New World in 1740. This Presley almost certainly originated from East Anglia, where the name is still fairly common today. Further confirmation of this link can be found in the record number of early settlers from this part of England who sailed to America in the pioneer days, and who gave the names of their old towns (such as Ipswich, Chelmsford and Groton) to the new communities they founded.

Vernon Presley toiled in the fields for a local landowner, and Gladys supplemented his meagre income by working in a factory. Their home was what is generally referred to as a 'shotgun shack' – so small (ten feet wide by thirty feet long) that, according to the origin of the phrase, you could stand on the front porch and fire a gun in the door and through the two rooms and out of the back before the buckshot had spread out far enough to hurt anything!

East Tupelo was, as more than one commentator has said, a sorry excuse of a place for folks to live in. 'The good people of the Hill Country,' wrote one of them, Thomas McNamee, 'learned resignation, mysticism and civility; the bad ones resentment, alcohol and violence.'

The Great Depression which had swamped America from the day in October 1929 when share prices had tumbled unbelievably on the New York Stock Exchange, left its scar on the nation for years: perhaps nowhere more deeply than in the South. With unemployment running rife and the market having dropped out of commodities, what chance was there for the Southern sharecropper and his family? Indeed, starvation and ruin were staring them in the face in 1933 when the new President, Franklin D. Roosevelt, came to office. But at least he had a very definitely stated intention: 'If dire need on the part of any of our citizens makes necessary the appropriation of additional funds . . . I shall not hesitate to authorise that expenditure.'

And authorise it he did. What Roosevelt put into operation was a bold new programme of experimentation

Elvis left the poverty of the South to become a world super-star – as exemplified in these shots from *Wild In The Country* and *Elvis On Tour*.

The Memorial Highway which links Tupelo and Memphis and on which Elvis travelled from rags to riches.

to get the country back on its feet – the 'New Deal' it was called – and the desperate South was one of the first parts of the country to benefit. The Tennessee Valley Authority was created which harnessed the mighty Tennessee River to bring new life to the poverty stricken areas along its banks through the power of hydroelectricity, as well as setting up a programme of soil conservation, reforestation and industrialisation.

The town councillors of Tupelo seized this God (and man) given opportunity and were the very first community in the area to contract with the Authority for electricity. Their reward was to see the beginnings of what would ultimately turn the town into a prosperous community.

But as can happen with prosperity, it did not bring relief to all the citizens, and by and large, those 'across the tracks' in East Tupelo did not greatly benefit. Vernon and Gladys Presley struggled on to feed and clothe themselves and their growing son for thirteen more years before deciding there really was no future for them in this neck of the woods. It was time to move on, they decided, and the place they chose to go to was the city of Memphis, one hundred miles north-west along Highway 78.

The family's departure was not even noticed, and probably today no one in Tupelo would even be able to recall them had it not been for the astonishing fame the boy Elvis later achieved.

In the typical Southern town which has grown in the wake of the Tennessee Valley Authority's work, the signs of his life here are now very evident. Indeed, a suspiciously large number of the population of 20,000 people 'claim' to have known the Presleys – but this should not be allowed to detract from the fame Elvis has brought to his birthplace.

The entire area around the little 'shotgun' shack has been transformed. Some years back the city acquired fifteen acres of land and turned it into a parkland with special facilities including a swimming pool and a youth centre, for teenagers and young children. It is most appropriately called the Elvis Presley Park and attracts thousands of visitors every year.

Old Saltillo Road, the dirt track which ran by the shack, has now been properly laid out and renamed Elvis Presley Drive, while the surrounding bluffs are known as Elvis Presley Heights. The little homestead was taken over in 1973 by the East Tupelo Garden Club whose members painted and refurbished it, complete with furniture from the Depression era of the type the Presleys had. (It is

The little weatherboard shack on Old Saltillo Road, Tupelo where Elvis was born.

interesting to learn that Elvis several times revisited his old home – usually at night, for obvious reasons – and once brought his daughter, Lisa Marie, to see it. His last visit to Tupelo was, in fact, only the month before he died.)

The home is now a State Historical Monument and is generally considered the centrepiece of the whole area, although the Elvis Presley Memorial Chapel, which stands nearby, is very popular with visitors. How this building came to be opened in 1979 has been explained by Mrs Jannelle McComb, the moving spirit behind its construction and a long-time friend of the Presley family.

'Elvis was immensely proud of his accomplishments,' she said, 'but he never forgot his humble beginnings, and he was mighty pleased when his old home was renovated. Once, when I was showing him some pictures of the work, I asked him what he would like if anything was ever set up in his memory in Tupelo. For a moment he stopped, and then he said, "Why don't you build a chapel so my fans can go and meditate and reflect on their lives and know that no matter what station they reach in life, if they place their talent in the hands of God, he can bless it and they can make a contribution to the world?"'

The result of this wish is now there for all to see: a twelve-hundred-square-foot chapel with a redwood exterior, complete with sixteen stained glass windows and furnishings donated by Elvis' associates and fans. One clear glass window on the northwest side looks directly out on the birthplace just a hundred feet away.

The most grandiose tribute to his name is certainly the renaming of Highway 78, the arterial road which runs from Tupelo to Memphis and along which the Presley family travelled in their beaten-up old car in September 1948. It is now known as the Elvis Aaron Presley Memorial Highway.

As he drove along this self-same highway all those years ago, Vernon Presley expressed his belief that Memphis offered Gladys and 13-year-old Elvis more of a future. Neither he (nor Elvis for that matter) had a bad word then or at any time for Tupelo: they just yearned for better things. How right Vernon's decision proved to be surpassed even his wildest dreams.

It was in Memphis, of course, that Elvis met his moment of destiny when he recorded that fateful little disc singing 'That's All Right, Mama', as a birthday present for Gladys, and thereby set in motion the chain of events which were to make him the most famous entertainer of the twentieth century.

Memphis may well have attracted Vernon Presley as the 'promised land', but its history certainly belied any such description. Disputed by the British, French and Spanish in the eighteenth century, it had been laid out in 1819 by Andrew Jackson, although his high ideals for it were not sustained and it became a 'tough and uninviting place overrun by the scum of the river', according to one account. A plague of yellow fever in 1878 did nothing to help its growth. But then suddenly, at the turn of the century, the development of cotton and lumber industries saw it rapidly boom into the second largest city in the South, with a population of more than 100,000. It still retained its unsavoury elements, however; crime and corruption leeched onto the boom and, by the 1920s, turned it into the 'Murder Capital' of the nation.

A crusading mayor named Edward Hull Crump proved the saviour of the city, although it took his particular form of benevolent dictatorship to turn the tide. He was, however, the first man to give consideration to the needs of the negro families who now made up forty per cent of the population. Among these thousands of blacks who had poured into the city from the surrounding rural areas were numerous talented musicians, including the legendary W.C. Handy, 'father of the blues', who played the piano in a saloon on Beale Street and immortalised the city in song.

It was to this selfsame Beale Street that young Elvis was drawn not long after settling in the city. His interest had been caught by the black rhythm and blues music he heard from local radio stations, and he sought out the real thing.

Graceland, the mansion style house in Memphis, which fame and fortune brought for Elvis.

13

His absorption of this music, plus the gospel songs he heard in church, and Country & Western ('the poor whites' blues', one critic called it) gave him the raw material for his own style.

Just as Mayor Crump transformed the character of Memphis and W.C. Handy captured its soul in song, so Elvis has imprinted his achievement on it. His name adorns buildings, monuments, roads and numerous souvenir shops and restaurants. Indeed, to the faithful it is Elvis Presley City in all but name – while Graceland, the impressive mansion which he bought when fame embraced him and where he lived for the rest of his life, is the very heart of the legend, a place now of pilgrimage for all fans.

Although Vernon Presley and his family doubtless needed directions when they first arrived in Memphis thirty and more years ago, such things are superfluous today when looking for Graceland. The old Highway 51 South on which the house stands is now called Elvis Presley Boulevard, and sign posts with a logo of the singer holding a microphone point the way. And as if that is not enough, a large barrage balloon bearing the words 'Graceland Free Parking' hangs overhead.

It was in March 1957 that Elvis bought the 18-room mansion in just over 13 acres of parkland at 3764, Elvis Presley Boulevard, when it was being used as a church serving the South Memphis suburb of Whitehaven. Then the area was sparsely populated, but by 1969, when it was formally incorporated into the city of Memphis, it was ringed by developments and shopping precincts. Today it is completely surrounded by every possible manifestation of the Presley phenomenon, from gift shops to a pink upholstered restaurant called 'Heartbreak Hotel'.

Elvis, of course, changed the interior of Graceland almost beyond recognition, and now it is the highlight of a coach tour which also stops in the city to look at Sun Records and the Elvis Presley Statue in Beale Street.

Walking into Graceland, up the sweep of gravel driveway and through the tall colonnades at the front of the mansion, and from there into the white-carpeted hallway, is like walking into another world – the world of 'The King' – which visitors must find as great a contrast to their own homes as Elvis did when he thought back to his old homestead in Tupelo. To call it a palace is no overstatement.

The whole interior of the house is opulent, with gold-fringed peacock-blue curtaining over the windows and archways, and mirrors just about everywhere. By way of introduction, a huge oil painting of Elvis hangs in the hall, as well as one of those instantly recognisable and haunting close-up photographs taken when he was 21.

Then comes the extensive drawing room, decorated in white, blue and gold, and at the end, Elvis' massive gold-plated Kimball piano, said to be worth $500,000, on which he played contentedly for hours on end.

Next is Elvis' den with three televisions, rows of books (mainly of a religious and inspirational nature) and his collection of guns. In the trophy room hangs his army uniform, his honourable discharge and a framed petition from thousands of fans begging the authorities not to call him up!

Beyond these rooms is what has been called 'the most impressive hallway you will ever see in your life.' It is a passageway with gold discs mounted in sparkling rows from floor to ceiling, almost as far as the eye can see, commemorating Elvis' incredible record sales of more than 800 million copies (and still growing!).

Outside the house, at the back, is a carport containing a selection of Elvis' cars: pride of place going to the pink 1955 Fleetwood Cadillac he bought for his mother at the onset of his fame. Also standing in the serried ranks are a magnificent Stutz Bluehawk, originally ordered for Frank Sinatra, and a 1967 black Dino Ferrari.

Finally, the visitor reaches the Garden of Meditation where Elvis lies beside his mother and father, along with a little tablet commemorating Jessie Garon, his twin brother who was still-born. The graves are set in a circular-walled and Doric-pillared plaza with a fountain playing in the centre and a statue of Christ, arms raised. This shrine has been a mass of flowers since the day Elvis was laid to rest.

These rows of multi-coloured bouquets which are placed day in and day out bear silent witness to the devotion and esteem of Elvis' fans, the fans who will celebrate the 50th anniversary of his birth with the same dedication that they have celebrated all the others these past thirty years since he sprang to fame. And no matter what attempts have been made to besmirch the Presley legend – or indeed may well be made in the future – the message is still clear: 'The King Lives.'

For when Elvis and his folks travelled those one hundred miles from Tupelo to Memphis, they did not just move to a new life. They travelled into immortality.

Elvis Presley Park and Elvis Presley Center in Tupelo which now draw thousands of fans every year.

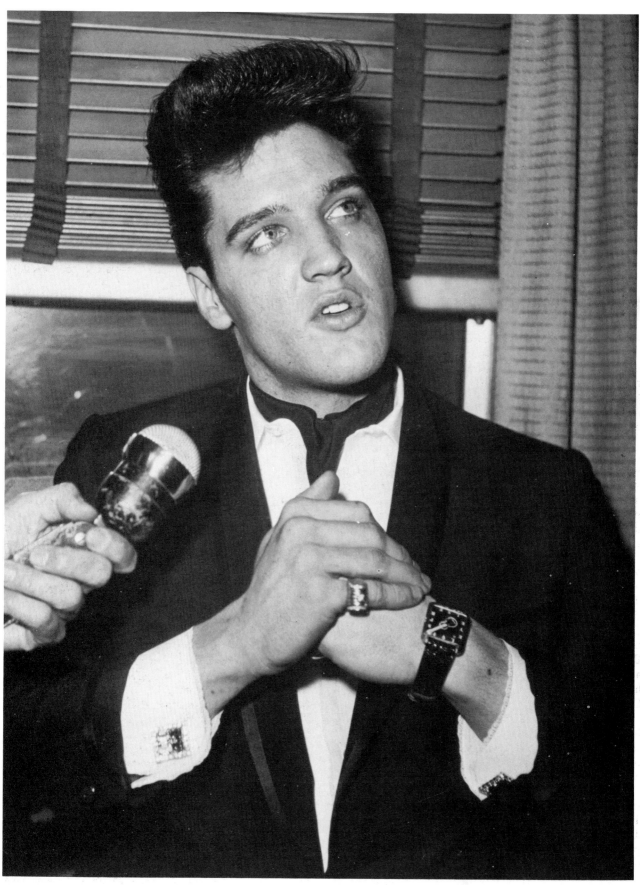

Elvis being interviewed early in his career.

'I Wanted to be a Truck Driver'

Elvis' own comments on his rise to
fame: from interviews 1956–1976

'Those early years were wild, man. They were the
good old days – the very best years.'

'I guess it all begins with my Mama. She was much more
than a mother – she was a friend I could talk to, any hour
of the day or night. Often I would get mad when she would
not let me do things I wanted, but she always knew best as
it turned out.

'I often resented not being allowed to go playing down
the creek with the other kids. Sometimes I'd run off and my
Mama would whup me and I'd go to bed crying, thinking
that she didn't love me. But she did.

'When I was a little kid we used to go to these church
meetings where there was a lot of singing. There were these
perfectly fine singers, but nobody responded to them. Then
there were the preachers and they cut up all over the place,
jumping on the piano, moving every which way. The
audience liked them. I guess I learned a lot from them.

'When I was growing up (in the nineteen forties), I
listened to the radio a lot and my favourite programmes
were those with the blues singers and the country music
singers – the *Grand Ole Opry* in particular. I guess my first
actual singing was in church. I loved the gospel singing – I
still do. Originally, I wanted to join a gospel group, because
my mother wanted me to sing gospel. I also sang at school
and sometimes for my friends.

'My Mama taught me some songs from a little old
Western folk song book she had bought. I used to sing along
with the radio, too. That's the way I learned a lot of songs.
Then I'd get to fooling around, giving my own interpreta-
tion and expressing the songs with my own feelings. My
Daddy could play a banjo, and he'd keep threatening to
buy me a guitar someday so we could accompany ourselves.
But there was never that much money around loose. I saw
a guitar one time in a store window for $12.50. I'd like to
have bought it, but I might just as well have tried to buy
City Hall.

'When I was a teenager I was the only one with long
hair. All the others had crewcuts. I think they all thought I
was some kind of freak. I wore loud clothes. The blacks, the
reds and the pinks. I guess I was different even then. I was
way out.

'I suppose I sometimes dreamed about being an entertainer, but I never thought it would turn out the way it did.
To begin with, I hadn't the remotest idea of a career. I
didn't plan it. When I was twelve I thought it would be
great driving a truck because I like driving. Later, I always
reckoned if music failed I could go back to truck driving!

'I guess the first time I realised there was money in
singing was after I went down to Sun Records and made
that first record, "My Happiness" and "That's When Your
Heartaches Begin". A year later Sam Phillips called me to
see what we could cook up. I suppose it was then I realised
that I might have a future if people would pay me to sing.

'After I had cut a few records for Sun, Colonel Parker
came into my life. He said he'd heard my records and that
I needed a business manager. He said I'd make more money
singing than trucking. He signed me along with Scotty
[Moore] and Bill [Black] and we played around the country
driving from town to town. I was called "The Hillbilly
Cat".

'We spent a lot of time on the road in those early days,
but we never had enough money for things. We pooled our
money for hamburgers and many times we slept in our cars
because we didn't have the money for a hotel. Sometimes
we'd drive all night to get to where we were performing,
and as soon as we'd finished, drive all night again to the
next show.

'We had a lot of problems with transportation. The cars
would break down, and then we'd have to put what little
money we had saved into a new car so we could get to the
next job. There were even times when the cars would break
down and we'd have to hitch-hike or wire for the money
for a bus ride! It was very hard work, and there were times
I thought I should quit and go back to being an electrician
like my Daddy said. But I loved the crowds, the people, the
applause.

'I was scared the first time I performed live. I knew I
could do it if I could just get out there. And when I did, the
people were screaming and carrying on and it scared me
some more. I thought they didn't like me! And when I went
off they told me the crowd was yelling at my wiggling. Yet
the wiggling was just my natural movement to the music as
well as a bit of nervousness. I have to move or else I can't
sing right. I never did anything dirty; I was just responding
to the music.

'I learned later that Colonel Parker had been fixing the
audiences a little bit for the publicity. He'd given these
little girls that hung around a couple of dollars and free
tickets to the show to scream. But he soon found out that
they were going to scream anyway, so he didn't need to pay
them!

'I wasn't exactly an overnight success. It was a lot of hard
work early on. Travelling, sleepless nights – three years at
least. It made me very nervous, hyper-tense, and I often
found it very difficult to sleep with all my emotions pent-
up. And because the girls would have torn me apart, I
couldn't go out to relax. I just had to stay in hotel rooms. It
was very frustrating for a guy of 19.

'I remember some of the little towns we played. Usually,
they'd be having a country fair, and the stage would be set
up on a platform or a flat truck in the middle of town. We'd

go on after the local talent and I'd sing my records. The crowd would be all around the stage, men and women, babies and dogs, all making a terrible din. And there would be a bunch of girls right at the very front all freaking out.

'When I sang I'd be doing my usual thing trying to get them to scream louder. Then they'd try to get up on the stage, and I'd have to push them back with my foot. But I couldn't hold them back, and soon they would be on the stage, pulling at my clothes. Then I had to get off quick and

they would have to hide me in a store or filling station until things quietened down.

'There were times when I thought we would never get away from those girls. And there were times when we almost didn't – and I had to go to hospital for treatment to cuts and bruises.

'I think the worst moment was in Kansas City. I walked out of this back door and there were 30 screaming girls. They just dived on me and shredded this new sports coat I

(*Opposite*) 'A young boy with long hair and loud clothes' – but what a future lies ahead!

Elvis greeting fans with the elusive Colonel Tom Parker (on the extreme right) who masterminded his rise to fame.

The boy who dreamed of being a truck driver ended up with a fleet of cars – he is here seen at the wheel of one of his first Cadillacs.

had just bought. Also my shirt and pants and underwear! Before the police rescued me I was left with only one shoe and one sock. Everything else was gone – even a lot of skin. They had to put iodine all over me in hospital. And because I'm allergic to iodine, I came all out in a rash!

'I have never been afraid of my audiences, just of what can happen in a crowd. I don't think anyone means to hurt you. They just want to be near you, to shake hands, or maybe touch you. But then something happens and it all gets out of control. Then I am frightened. But that doesn't mean I don't love the fans and singing for them. It's my life. It's what I'm here for. It's all I want to do as long as they want me to do it. After all, I owe everything to them.

'After I signed with RCA Records, the first thing I did was to buy my Mama a Cadillac. A pink one. That was her dream when she was scrubbing floors and cleaning up at the hospital where she was working. She often saw a fine lady drive up in a big Cadillac. She told me about her. Mama was never one to want or ask for anything for herself. But I knew how thrilled a car like that would make her. Besides she was the finest lady God ever put on earth. I didn't know for sure how long we could afford to keep it, but I knew one thing – she was going to have it. Then when the big money came, I bought her a house.

'When I was on tour I'd call Mama every night without fail. She worried constantly about me when I was on the

road and could never go to sleep before I'd telephoned. She didn't think I was taking enough care of myself.

'She got a bit upset when she came to a few of my concerts and saw the crowds mobbing me. The girls tearing at my clothes and the guys threatening me. The boyfriends of my girl fans hated me. I could never understand it. They were always trying to pick fights. Having a smack at me. Most of the time I'd just have to ride it. Nothing else you could do. Occasionally, I got real mad and defended myself extra good, if you see what I mean.

'Anyhow, I told my Mama that it was going to keep on happening, for a while anyhow. And as long as it did, the money would keep coming in. She also didn't like it when people called me 'Elvis the Pelvis' – and nor did I. I mean it's one of the most childish expressions I ever heard coming from an adult – but if they *want* to call me that, I guess there's nothing I can do about it, so I just have to accept it. You have to accept the good with the bad, the bad with the good.

'I don't think my actions on stage are vulgar. I know that I get carried away with the music and the beat sometimes, and I don't know quite what I'm doing. But it is all rhythm and beat – full of life.

'The kids come to have a good time. I don't see why they should call them idiots. After all, they're somebody's kids, probably raised in decent homes, too. If they want to pay their money and come and jump around and scream and yell, it's their business. They'll grow up some day and grow out of that.

'Some of the adults are understanding. They come around to me and say, "I don't like your kind of music, but my kids like it, and I haven't got any kick about it because when I was young I liked the Charleston and the Foxtrot."

'I'll tell you, live audiences are my favourite – pictures next, then television. When I go on that stage before thousands of kids I'm like any performer. I feel really good. People say I inspire the riots that go on when I sing. That isn't true. But there isn't a performer who doesn't like that wild acceptance. It's a good feeling . . . and if it's really loud it covers up my mistakes!

'I believe that when you are on stage you have to put on a show for people. If I just stood and sung and never moved, people would say, "Hey, what am I doing here? I could stay at home and listen to his records!" You have to give them something to come out for and talk about.

'I know it may sound funny, but I'm shy. I don't talk easily with strangers. I get so I don't know what to say to people. So when they want me to meet lots of people I try to get out as quickly as I can.

'I don't think success has changed me inside. Only thing, sometimes I feel like I'm sixteen years old, and it seems like I'm a little kid that has to have someone watch over me. The other times I feel like I'm grown up and have been around – which I have. It scares the hell out of me, those feelings. I guess I'll never grow old.

'One time, my Daddy and me were talking about what happened. He looked at me and said, "What happened, El? The last thing I remember is I was working in a paint factory and you was driving a truck." And I remember how, after something big happened along about 1957, I was sitting at home and found my Mama staring at me. I asked her why, and she just shook her head and said, "I don't believe it. I just don't believe it." And I guess I feel that same way.'

The proud owner of Graceland stands at the ornate front gates.

Sources: *Time, Newsweek, Life, Billboard, Variety, Los Angeles Times, New York Times, News of the World, Daily Express, Daily Mirror, Sunday Dispatch, Evening News, Evening Standard, Sunday Times, Record Mirror, New Musical Express*, Jerry Hopkins, May Mann, Ed Parker, Becky Yancey, Todd Slaughter, and the recollections of fans at Elvis' concerts.

Elvisology

Fifty Remarkable Years: 1935–1985

1935

January 8, 1935. In a two-roomed 'shotgun-style' shack on Old Saltillo Road in East Tupelo, amidst the cotton fields of Mississippi, a son to be named Elvis Aaron Presley is born to a farm worker, Vernon Elvis Presley, and his sewing machine operator wife, Gladys (née Smith), who had been married on June 17, 1933. The boy is the second of twins, and his birth at 4.35 am on a bitterly cold morning has been overshadowed by the still-birth thirty-five minutes earlier of another son who is given the name of Jessie Garon before being buried in a tiny, unmarked grave in the nearby Priceville Cemetery. The birth certificate for Elvis (reproduced opposite) shows only one year's difference in the age of his parents – when in fact there was four – and spells his middle name with only one 'a', though it was ever after to be given with two. Although the tiny shack in which Elvis is born (built by his father with a loan of $180 from his employer, Orville Bean) is less than thirty feet long, has no running water and only a single electrical point, it is filled with love as Gladys Presley devotes all her time and her affection to her surviving son.

1937

Spring, 1937. Elvis is being raised as a polite, respectful child never out of his mother's sight. He is taken to church by his religious-minded parents and at the First Assembly of God Church on Adams Street, East Tupelo, develops the love of music which is to shape his life. Mrs Gladys Presley recalls these formative events: 'When Elvis was just a little fellow he would slide off my lap, run down the aisle and stand looking up at the choir. He would try and sing with them, and though he was too little to know the words, he could carry the tune.' As he grows up, Elvis joins in with his parents at the lively, often noisy meetings of song and prayer which typify this revivalist-style of Church. The joy of these meetings temporarily makes the Presleys forget the harsh poverty of their day-to-day lives.

1938

May 25, 1938. The Presleys' hardships are increased when Vernon Presley is given a three-year jail sentence after pleading guilty to a minor crime of forgery. He is indicted with his wife's brother, Travis Smith, and a friend, Luther Gable, of altering a cheque made out by his employer, Orville Bean. Though the crime was evidently committed as a result of a dire need of money, the three men are each sentenced to three years in the infamous hard-labour Parchman Penitentiary, the state prison of Mississippi. Because of his good behaviour and hard work, Vernon Presley is released just over a year later: but in the meantime Gladys and her young son (now three years old) have been turned out of the shack they rented from Orville Bean, and Elvis has developed a fear of losing either his father or his mother which is never to leave him.

1940

January, 1940. Now turned five, Elvis begins his education at the East Tupelo Consolidated School, a basic wood-frame building housing several hundred pupils in the charge of two dozen teachers taking them through all twelve grades. Gladys Presley walks her son to and from school, and there he proves a quiet, well-behaved, though no more than average pupil. Only his voice makes an impression on his teacher, Mrs J. C. Grimes: 'Each morning we had chapel and he sang several songs on various occasions. I remember one of them and it wasn't really right for chapel, but Elvis sang it so sweetly it almost made me cry.'

1945

October 3, 1945. Because of his singing, the School Principal, Mr J. D. Cole, enters Elvis in a talent contest at the annual Mississippi–Alabama Fair and Dairy Show. Ten years old, he sings an old favourite about a boy and his dog, 'Old Shep', unaccompanied and standing on a chair to reach the microphone. For what is to prove a rare moment in his life, he has to take second place – to a six-year-old girl, Becky Harris, singing the blues song, 'Sentimental Journey'. Elvis' prize is five dollars and free admission to all the amusement rides. (Interestingly, he is to return to this self-same event in 1957 to sing again and also receive the key to Tupelo, presented by the Governor of Mississippi, James P. Coleman.) Unsure though the rendering of 'Old Shep' is, it still marks Elvis' first public performance, and because it is also broadcast over the local radio station, WELO, his first broadcast, too. He will later record the Red Foley song in Hollywood in September 1956.

1946

January 8, 1946. Elvis' interest in music intensifies, particularly the gospel and black music he listens to on the radio, and for his birthday he is given a guitar, bought for $12.75 by his mother from the Tupelo Hardware Company. (According to one story, Elvis would have preferred a bicycle or a gun, but his mother was afraid he might hurt himself with either and so talked him into having the guitar.) He is taught to play the instrument by his uncles, Johnny Smith and Vester Presley, as well as listening to the radio. 'I learned most of it from the radio station in Tupelo,' he says later, 'and from other people's phonograph records.'

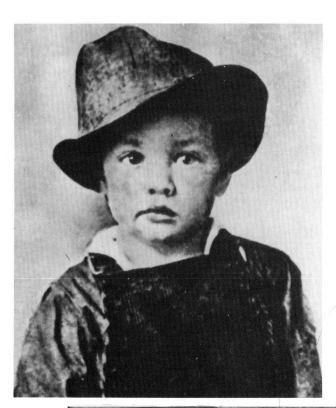

The earliest known photograph of Elvis at 2-years-old with (*below*) a facsimile of his birth certificate.

1947

June, 1947. The still impoverished Presleys have by now moved into Tupelo itself where they first occupy a slum house in Commerce Street and then close to the railway tracks in Mobile Alley. While Vernon Presley drives a truck, Elvis attends Milam Junior High School. Here a classmate, James Ausborn, has a brother who is a professional singer named Mississippi Slim, and Elvis frequently watches him perform at radio station WELO which is based in Mobile Alley.

1948

September, 1948. Times become desperate for Vernon Presley when he loses his job. With a wife and a teenage son to support, he decides to leave Tupelo and move 100 miles across the Tennessee border to Memphis where he had once worked during the years of World War II. It is a traumatic journey for Elvis as he later recalls. 'We were broke, man, broke,' he says. 'So we left Tupelo overnight. Dad packed

---

DEPARTMENT OF COMMERCE
Bureau of The Census

STANDARD CERTIFICATE OF LIVE BIRTH
STATE OF MISSISSIPPI

State File Number

Registrar's SOUVENIR Number

PLACE OF BIRTH—
County *Lee* City or Town *Tupelo* Inside or Outside Corporate Limits *Inside*
Hospital *at home* or Street and No. *Old Saltilla Rd* or Rural Precinct

Mother's Stay Before Delivery—(a) In Hospital *at home* (b) In the Community *Yes*

2. RESIDENCE OF MOTHER—
State *Miss* County *Lee* City or Town *Tupelo* or Rural Precinct

3. FULL NAME OF CHILD *Elvis Aron Presley* 4. DATE OF BIRTH *1-8-35*

5. Boy or Girl? *Boy* 6. Twin or Triplet? *Twin* If born 1st, 2d, or 3d 7. Number Months of Pregnancy *9* 8. Is Mother Married? *Yes*

FATHER OF CHILD

9. Full Name *Vernon Elvis Presley*
10. Color or Race *White* 11. Age at Time of this Birth *20* Yrs.
12. Where Born? *Mississippi*
13. Usual Occupation *Laborer*
14. Industry or Business

MOTHER OF CHILD

15. Full Maiden Name *Gladys Love*
16. Color or Race *White* 17. Age at Time of this Birth *21* Yrs.
18. Where Born? *Mississippi*
19. Usual Occupation *Factory Worker*
20. Industry or Business

21. CHILDREN BORN TO THIS MOTHER
(a) How many other children of this mother are now living? *None*

(b) How many other children were born alive but are now dead? *0* (c) How many children were born dead? *1*

22. Mother's Mailing Address for Registration Notice *Old Saltilla Rd.*

23. I hereby certify that I attended the birth of this child who was born alive at the hour of _____ M. on the date above stated, and that the information given was furnished by *Vernon Presley* related to this child as *father*

24. Date Rec'd. by Registrar
25. Signature of Registrar

(Signed) *Vernon Presley*
Address *Tupelo*

Elvis as a teenager: Aged 13 (*above*), second from left in the check shirt with three Memphis friends; aged 17 (*left*) on the back step of his home in Lauderdale Courts; and aged 19 when fame was just around the corner . . .

all our belongings in our 1937 Plymouth and we just headed for Memphis. He figured things just had to get better.' In Memphis, with its population of over 300,000, the family move into a one-room apartment at 572, Poplar Avenue, and Elvis is enrolled on the 16th at the huge and unsettling Humes High School with its total of over 1,600 pupils.

1949

May 1, 1949. The year proves more promising for the family. In February Vernon gets a job working for the United Paint Company, packing boxes of house paint, with a salary of $35 plus overtime. The couple also apply to the Memphis Housing Authority for better accommodation and after assessment are given a two-bedroom, ground floor flat at 328, Lauderdale Courts, a project building on Winchester Street. After a while, Vernon's mother, Minnie Mae, joins the family, and Elvis nick-names her affectionately, 'Dodger'. She is to stay close to him for the rest of his life. Although still shy, the teenager is gradually adjusting to city life and has taken to entertaining his friends by playing his guitar and singing. Half a mile away from where he plays is Beale Street, the legendary home of the blues . . .

1950

September, 1950. Elvis has developed a passion for American football (which is to remain with him throughout his life) and for a year is a member of the Humes High Tigers, playing defence. A leading member of the team is Bobby 'Red' West with whom Elvis becomes very friendly. According to Red, Elvis is a skilful, determined player, but the following year clashes with the team coach, Rube Boyce, about the length of his hair. When Elvis refuses to have it cut he is dropped from the team.

November, 1950. Elvis helps supplement the family income by getting a job as a cinema usher at Loew's State Cinema on South Main Street, Memphis, where he works a five hour shift for a weekly pay cheque of $12.75. Watching endless films in between showing patrons to their seats, he develops a great admiration for one of the hottest new movie stars, Tony Curtis, in particular his hair style. Elvis himself later adopts Curtis's distinctive 'duck tail' style.

1951

February, 1951. As well as his school work and the usher's job at Loew's State Cinema, Elvis gets another spare time job at the Marl Metal Company in Georgia Avenue, Memphis. This is tough, demanding labour, working from 3 pm to 11.30 pm for one dollar per hour. The strain of all his commitments leaves Elvis exhausted, and when his school work begins to suffer as a result, his mother insists he give up the jobs.

An intimate shot of the Presleys at home.

1952

December, 1952. Elvis makes his second public appearance when a teacher at Humes, Miss Elsie Scrivener, encourages him to perform at the annual Christmas concert. Perhaps not surprisingly, he chooses to repeat 'Old Shep' and such is the applause from the audience that he encores with 'Cold, Cold Icy Fingers'. He is so surprised at the response, he can only gasp to his teacher, 'They really liked me, Miss Scrivener – they really *liked* me!' Outside school, Elvis has attended his first gospel concert at Ellis Auditorium and formed an immediate admiration for the famous Blackwood Brothers; their lively, colourful and exhibitionist performances give him the urge to be a gospel singer. He hangs around the Auditorium to talk to the singers and for a time gets a job selling soft drinks so that he can watch the shows. There is also a tiny bit of fame for Elvis when he takes part in a 'Road-E-O' competition devised by the Junior Chamber of Commerce in Memphis to show contestants' skill with motor vehicles, and his photograph changing a tyre appears in the local paper. Occasionally, too, he entertains friends by singing and playing his guitar in Lauderdale Courts . . .

It was on the back of flatbed trucks like this one recreated in *Loving You* that Elvis, Scotty and Bill first performed publicly from 1954 onwards.

1953

April, 1953. Seeking to give his mother something different for her birthday on the 25th, Elvis decides to put his feelings for her into the form of a little record which he knows he can make at the Memphis Recording Service, 706, Union Avenue. He has passed this small studio many times while driving his truck and mentally registered the advertising claim, 'We Record Anything – Anywhere – Anytime'. Aside from this, the owner of the studio, Sam Phillips, 30, is fascinated by rhythm and blues and has launched a record label, Sun, to develop this interest commercially. Elvis goes into the studio on a hot Saturday afternoon, and for the price of four dollars records two songs on a ten-inch acetate disc, 'My Happiness' by Betty Peterson and Barney Bergentine and 'That's When Your Heartaches Begin' by Fred Fisher and Billy Hill, accompanying himself on his guitar. Although Elvis thinks the result sounds like 'somebody beating on a bucket lid', the receptionist at the studios, Marion Keisker, is impressed enough to tape part

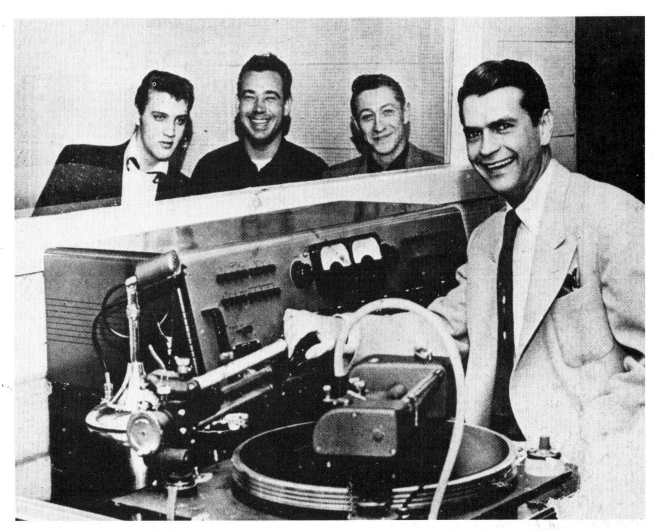

Sam Phillips in his very basic recording studio with Elvis, Bill and Scotty.

of the recording and make a note of the singer's name as 'Elvis Pressley'. Gladys Presley is delighted with the gift and – according to Elvis – 'borrowed a record player and played it over and over until it was plumb wore out.'

June, 1953. Elvis graduates from Humes High, and the school yearbook, *The Herald*, indicates he has majored in Engineering, History and English, with ROTC, and the clubs for English, History, Speech and Biology being his favourite activities. A cryptic comment beneath his photograph reads: 'Donald Williams, Raymond McCraig and Elvis Presley leave hoping there will be someone to take their places as "teacher's pets"????' As all three young men like singing, this is taken as an indication of their impact on the staff as musicians rather than being well-behaved! Because Gladys is now working as a nurse's aide at St Joseph's Hospital, the combined wage of the family forces them to leave subsidised Lauderdale Courts and they take an apartment at 398, Cypress Street.

July, 1953. 18-year-old Elvis gets his first full-time job at the Precision Tool Company, thanks to the help of two uncles already working there, and finds himself on an assembly line helping make shells for the army. He hates the repetitious work, and applies for a position at the Crown Electric Company, an electrical contracting firm. As he has learned to drive, he is soon given a chance to drive a truck taking supplies to the electricians at work on sites all over Memphis. His admiration for truck drivers is reflected in his appearance and the long sideburns which he cultivates. He has not lost his enthusiasm for music, however, and entertains friends and acquaintances, though he gets no encouragement from his father, as he is later to remember. 'My daddy knew a lot of guitar players, and most of them didn't work, and he said I must make up my mind to be either a guitar player or an electrician. He also said that he'd never seen a guitar player that was worth a damn!'

1954

January 4, 1954. In the week before his 19th birthday, Elvis returns to the Memphis Recording Service to make another four-dollar disc. This time owner Sam Phillips is in charge of the studio and recalls the young visitor's name from the tape made by his assistant. He listens with interest as Elvis

Two rare photographs at the very start of his career; (*left*) with his mother at home and (*below*) giving autographs to fans.

May, 1954. When Sam Phillips receives a demonstration disc of a song called 'Without You', he listens to the urgings of Marion Keisker to 'give the boy with the sideburns a chance to record it.' Elvis responds to her telephone call to come down to Union Avenue by reaching the recording studio almost before she has replaced the receiver. His performance is poor, however, and even when Phillips has him demonstrate other types of singing the results are unsatisfactory. He sees that the boy has promise, but needs experience, and decides to introduce him to two local musicians in the hope that the trio might come up with something recordable. The two men are Winfield Scott Moore, a guitar player two years older than Elvis, and William Black, a double bass player, aged 26. In the weeks that follow, Scotty Moore and Bill Black are slowly to forge a bond – and a sound – with Elvis which will lead first to the Sun recording studios and then unimaginable fame.

July 5, 1954. Believing they have found a rapport, Bill, Scotty and Elvis go into Sam Phillips' tiny studio on a sweltering summer evening. They begin by recording 'I Love You Because' and follow this with two country numbers, 'Harbour Lights' and 'Blue Moon'. Neither the trio nor Sam Phillips is particularly happy with any of the songs. The moment of record history which occurs next has been described by Scotty Moore. 'We were just sitting there, drinking coke, shooting the bull,' he says. 'Then Elvis picked up his guitar and started banging on it and singing "That's All Right, Mama". Jumping around the studio, just acting the fool. And Bill started beating on the bass and I joined in. Just making a racket we thought. The door to the control room was open, and when we were halfway through, Sam came running out and said, "What in the devil are you doing?" We said, "We don't know." And he said, "Well, find out real quick and don't lose it. Run through it again and let's put it on tape." So to the best of our knowledge we repeated what we had just done and went through the whole thing.' That tape of the tune by the black country blues singer, Arthur (Big Boy) Crudup is to create the phenomenon of Elvis Presley and remain an integral part of his performances for the rest of his life. Further recording sessions are required before a suitable song for the 'B' side of Elvis' first release is found – Bill Monroe's 'Blue Moon of Kentucky'.

July 7, 1954. In order to promote his record 'That's All Right, Mama', Sam Phillips plays the tape to his friend, Dewey Phillips, in the hope that he will use it on his popular late night radio show, 'Red, Hot and Blue', on WHBQ Memphis. He agrees – and Elvis himself has recalled what happens. 'I had Mama tune our radio into WHBQ, but I was too scared to stay and hear it. I went straight to a movie so I couldn't hear folks laughing at me, me pretending to be a somebody. I was really hiding in that movie scared. But when I got home, Mama grabbed me and hugged and kissed me – she was so excited and happy. She said the disc

records 'Casual Love Affair' and 'I'll Never Stand In Your Way'. He sees promise, but perhaps not the singer to fulfil his belief that, 'If I could find a white man who had the Negro sound and the Negro feel, I could make a billion dollars.' Sam does, though, take another note of Elvis' address – the family have moved again to 462, Alabama Street – and in answer to Elvis' questions says, yes, he will let him know if the chance to record commercially for Sun arises . . .

Edwin Howard

The Front Row

(Aug. 17, 1977)

Remembering How It All Began for Elvis . . .

THE MORNING of July 27, 1954, Marion Keisker (now Macinnes) phoned me from Sun Records, where she was Sam Phillips' right arm, and asked if she might bring a promising young Sun artist in to see me. Marion thought he had something. He had first come to Sun months before to use the studio's rental facilities to make a record for his mother on her birthday. Phillips had been intrigued and eventually recorded the boy commercially.

They would have to come in on the boy's lunch hour, Marion said, because he was still driving a truck for Crown Electric Co. I said I'd be glad to see them, and shortly after noon they got off the elevator on the fifth floor of *The Press-Scimitar* and came over to my desk.

The boy's hair looked as if it had been cut by a lawn mower, but the trademarks were already there — flat top, duck tail and sideburns. He was shy and, except for "Yes sir" and "No sir," let Marion do all the talking.

Here is the item that ran the next day in The Front Row — the first "interview" ever done with Elvis Presley:

IN A SPIN — Elvis Presley can be forgiven for going round and round in more ways than one these days. A 19-year-old Humes High graduate, he just signed a recording contract with Sun Record Co. of Memphis, and already has a disc out that promises to be the biggest hit that Sun has ever pressed.

ELVIS
First photo, 1954

It all started when Elvis dropped in to Sun's studios one day to cut a personal record at his own expense. Sam Phillips, president of the company, monitored the session and was so impressed with the unusual quality of the young man's voice that he jotted down his name and address. Some time later, Phillips came across a ballad which he thought might be right for Presley's voice. They recorded it; it didn't click. But they tried again, this time with "Blue Moon of Kentucky," a folk standard, backed by "That's All Right, Mama."

Just now reaching dealer's shelves, the record is getting an amazing number of plays on all Memphis radio stations. "The odd thing about it," says Marion Keisker of the Sun office, "is that both sides seem to be equally popular on pop, folk and race record programs. This boy has something that seems to appeal to everybody.

"We've just gotten the sample records out to the disc jockeys and distributors in other cities," she said, "but we got big orders yesterday from Dallas and Atlanta." Sun, started by Sam Phillips, former WREC engineer, several years ago, has 40 distributors from coast to coast, so there's a good chance of a big national sale.

Elvis, son of Mr. and Mrs. Vernon Presley, 462 Alabama, is a truck driver for Crown Electric Co. He has been singing and playing the guitar since he was about 13 — just picked it up himself. The home folks who have been hearing him on records so often during the past few weeks can see Elvis in person when he's presented by disc jockey Bob Neal in a hillbilly show at Overton Park Shell Friday night along with veteran entertainers from the Louisiana Hayride.

THE LATE Bob Johnson, television and later Good Evening columnist for *The Press-Scimitar*, took over the Elvis watch after that and wrote reams about him, covering his Las Vegas debut in 1955 and eventually commuting to New York to edit a magazine devoted primarily to Elvis, called *16*. I got back into the act occasionally, since I covered movies. I covered his last live show before going into the Army, and had a private interview with him in November of 1963 on the set of *Kissin' Cousins* at MGM.

"I guess the last time I really saw you was at the Tupelo Fair just before I went into the Army," he said as he sat down in his portable dressing room on the sound stage. "Gosh, an awful lot has happened since then. A lot of pictures, too. Let's see, this must be 11 since I got out.

"Yes I still enjoy it. I don't know — you get a little older and you get a little more adjusted to it. It gets to be just a job. I guess the biggest thing is the mental strain, trying to remember your lines and look your best, and all that.

"I don't have much time for anything else while I'm working. Work pretty late every night. But I do date Ann-Margret some."

THAT WAS THE LAST TIME I talked to Elvis, but of course I've kept up with him — and in recent years felt sorry for him. Not because he turned 40 and got fat. That was natural. The body matures and grows old.

What was sad to me was that imprisoned within that body was a child who never grew up. He made a huge fortune and might have done great good without depriving himself. He could have endowed hospitals, universities, research. Instead he gave nominally to varied charities and bought expensive cars for strangers — like an ordinary person tossing pennies to ragamuffins.

He might himself have traveled and studied and grown. Instead, he was content to go on playing the games of his youth — renting theaters and rinks and courts and amusements parks for private parties — playing pitch for kewpie dolls.

There was a time, after his return from Army service, when he began to blossom as an actor and might have developed into a fine one. But again he drew back and instead re-made again and again the same formula films. He never developed, never learned how to spend his money — or his time.

Middle age sat unseemly on him. Old age would have been obscene. His life had become so sad to me that his death seems less so.

jockey Dewey Phillips had so many telephone calls and even telegrams about my record that he had played it repeatedly. Well, it sold 7,000 in Memphis. I made several more, but they didn't seem to be good enough. I didn't make big time or set the world on fire. I thought it was just a one-time thing, and I concentrated on driving the truck. But I'd sing around at places and on local programmes when they'd ask me. Mama wanted me to. I knew it pleased her so I'd sing. And soon I was getting as much as ten dollars for my singing.' According to another version of this night, Gladys and Vernon Presley fetch their son from the Suzore No 2 cinema where he is hiding and take him to Dewey Phillips' studio to be interviewed. Apparently Elvis carries out what he believes is a preliminary run-through of the interview, only to find he has been on the air all the time! The response to the song causes Sam Phillips to advance his pressing date, and the record is released on July 19.

July 12, 1954. Sam Phillips suggests to Elvis that Scotty Moore act as his manager and booking agent, and the two sign a brief contract which gives Moore just ten per cent of the singer's earnings in return for his services.

July 28, 1954. The first 'interview' with Elvis is published in the local Memphis *Press-Scimitar* by columnist Edwin Howard, as a result of Marion Keisker introducing the two men during Elvis' lunch break from Crown Electrics! (See previous page.)

July 30, 1954. 'That's All Right, Mama' reaches number three on the Memphis C & W Chart, and Elvis makes his debut as a public performer at The Shell in Overton Park, accompanied by Scotty and Bill, and including in his segment, naturally enough, his 'hit' record. Naturally enough, too, he is very nervous. 'I was scared stiff,' he says later, 'it was my first big appearance in front of an audience. I came out and was doing a fast type tune, "Good Rockin' Tonight", and everybody was hollering, but I didn't know what they were hollering at. When I came off stage, Scotty told me, "It was the way you were shaking your left leg. That's what got them screaming." Well, I went back for an encore, and I kinda did a little more, and the more I wiggled, the wilder they got.' The sensational effect of this performance causes the star of the show, Webb Pierce, to exclaim, 'Sonofabitch!'

September 9, 1954. Elvis' famous 'wiggle' has been somewhat refined for greater impact when he and his accompanists appear at the opening of the Doug Katz Store in the Airways Shopping Centre in Memphis. The trio perform on a flatbed truck and the adults present are as amazed as the young people are delighted. In between their daytime jobs, Elvis, Scotty and Bill also record their next disc containing the already well-received 'Good Rockin' Tonight' and 'I Don't Care If The Sun Don't Shine'.

September 25, 1954. After vigorous promotion work, Sam Phillips manages to get Elvis a spot on the prestigious

The famous 'swivel' which helped make Elvis famous in 1954.

country music show, 'Grand Ole Opry', presented live from the Ryman Auditorium in Nashville and broadcast all over the American South and West by WSM Radio. Driving to Nashville, Elvis is first disappointed by the drab, rather

30

church-like appearance of the fabled Opry building and then by the refusal of the manager, Jim Denny, to let him sing his latest tunes (which happen to be released this day). Nor do things get better when he performs. His fusion of rhythm and blues and country music is not well received by the purist 'Grand Ole Opry' audience, and Jim Denny tells him bluntly, 'We don't do that kind of Negro music here. If I were you, I'd go back to truck driving.' It is a very despondent Elvis who returns to Memphis, his first – and last – appearance in the 'Mecca of Country Music' behind him.

October 16, 1954. Elvis' spirits are not down for long. 'That's All Right, Mama' actually reaches the number one spot in the Memphis charts – as well as selling well in New Orleans and even Nashville (eat your hearts out, Opry fans!) – and *Billboard* gives him his first and very complimentary review, describing him as 'a potent new chanter who can sock over a tune for either the country or the r & b markets.' Despite the poor reception he has received on the 'Grand Ole Opry', Sam Phillips is able to get Elvis a booking on another live radio show, 'Louisiana Hayride', only just second in popularity. At this Saturday night show from Shreveport, the teenager is given an excellent build-up and is a hit with listeners and 'Hayride' officials alike. He is immediately offered a contract to appear every week for the next year, and is soon the only regular on the show who can be guaranteed to fill all 3,500 seats in the auditorium when he appears. The trio are also getting bookings all over the area, although the money is still small and the travelling exhausting. But as Scotty Moore recalls, 'I think that was when we knew things were beginning to happen. It was obvious people were getting very receptive to what Elvis was doing – and for his part, he could work an audience to death.'

November, 1954. With the guarantee of the weekend booking on the 'Louisiana Hayride' and an ever-increasing demand to play one-night stands in Louisiana and Mississippi, Elvis quits his job at the Crown Electric Company and takes to the road – not altogether to the pleasure of his mother. The trio are also augmented by a piano player, D. J. Fontana, and the group becomes known as Elvis Presley and the Blue Moon Boys. Says D.J. later, 'Elvis was getting pretty hot in the area then, tearing down houses everywhere.'

December, 1954. Elvis, Scotty and Bill return to the Sun studio to cut another record, the evocative 'Baby Let's Play House' and 'You're A Heartbreaker'. Although only moderately successful in sales terms, the disc is somehow evocative of what is happening in Elvis' public appearances – for his direct sexual appeal is driving female audiences wild and causing mounting anger among the more jealous boyfriends of these girls. From Mississippi he receives what is to prove the first of a string of paternity suits – but like all the rest this claim by a besotted fan that Elvis has made her pregnant is speedily dismissed. In fact, he still has eyes for only one girl, Dixie Locke, a Memphis teenager he has been dating since his last year at Humes

An informal picture of Elvis getting ready to perform and (*below*) the famous Grand Ole Opry in Nashville which proved such a disappointment to Elvis.

Elvis' first major triumph on the 'Louisiana Hayride' – in this rare photograph of the artists who appeared on the show in 1954 he can be seen on the far right.

High, and who is to become the president of his first fan club.

1955

January 10, 1955. Shortly after his twentieth birthday – and with the agreement of Scotty Moore who has found playing and making business arrangements an impossible task – Elvis takes a new manager, Bob Neal, a well-known Memphis music personality. As he is still a minor, Vernon and Gladys Presley must approve the contract which gives Neal 15 per cent of the take. Neal immediately gets Elvis increased radio exposure and a wider range of bookings before better-paying audiences. Reports such as this from *Billboard* magazine become increasingly frequent: 'Info that Elvis Presley pulled a capacity crowd on the "Grand Prize Saturday Night Jamboree" at Eagles Hall, Houston.'

March 3, 1955. Another first for Elvis – he appears on television when NBC screen part of the 'Louisiana Hayride', but he is so fleeting as to pass unnoticed by most viewers. Nonetheless, Bob Neal is encouraged enough to have Elvis and the Blue Moon Boys fly to New York to audition for the 'Arthur Godfrey Talent Show', a popular television

showcase for new artists. But Elvis is clearly ahead of his time where the show is concerned and he is rejected. Elvis enjoys neither the flight to New York – his first – nor the city itself, so he returns South quite unperturbed and willing to bide his time . . .

May 1, 1955. Elvis and the Blue Moon Boys go on their first major tour as part of Hank Snow's All-Star Jamboree. Also on this three-week tour, which begins in New Orleans and goes through Louisiana, Alabama, Florida, Georgia, Virginia, North Carolina and Tennessee, are Faron Young, Slim Whitman, Mother Maybelle Carter and the Carter Sisters. Elvis has his new Sun record, 'Baby Let's Play House', to promote, and watching him perform – as well as the reaction of the audiences – is the part under-writer of the tour, a certain Colonel Tom Parker. According to a report in *Billboard,* 'Col. Parker, assisted by Tom Diskin, is using radio, TV, newspapers and circus billing to herald the mammoth show.' Aside from his natural interest in the show he has financed along with Hank Snow, the Colonel is interested in Elvis because he has been specially recommended to him as a rising star by one of his talent scouts, Whitey Ford, a country singer and comedian best known as 'The Duke of Paducah'.

June 24, 1955. At the 'Big D Jamboree' in Dallas, Texas, Elvis' manager, Bob Neal, meets Colonel Parker for the first time and they discuss the young singer's future. Parker,

By 1955, young girls were pursuing Elvis everywhere he went. Thousands of candid shots like this one are now the treasured possessions of fans all over America.

born in 1910 and believed to be of Dutch origin, has become renowned as a promoter and tough negotiator from his days working in carnivals; he promptly books Elvis into several other package tours he is organising.

June 25, 1955. With his rising popularity, Elvis achieves another life-long ambition by buying his first Cadillac. Although only secondhand and partly financed by Bob Neal, it is his pride and joy until disaster strikes, as *Billboard* reports: 'Elvis Presley saw red early last week when flames devoured his pretty pink Cadillac on the road between Hope and 'Texarkana, Ark ...' It is quickly replaced, however, by a new version, painted in Elvis' favourite colours, pink and black. There is also a pink and white Ford for his mother and father.

August 13, 1955. *Billboard* describes what is soon to become the norm at Elvis' appearances – a riot. 'Elvis Presley created pandemonium among the teenage country fans at Jacksonville, Florida recently, and before he could be rescued from his swooning admirers they had relieved him of his tie, handkerchieves, belt and the greater part of his coat and shirt.' Manager Bob Neal is equally amazed at what is happening. 'You'd see this frenzied reaction, particularly from the young girls,' he says. 'We hadn't gone out and arranged for anybody to squeal and scream. These girls screamed spontaneously. For a long time there'd been nobody who'd done that – not since Sinatra fifteen years earlier.'

August 15, 1955. With 'Baby Let's Play House' in the Country Top Ten, Sun release Elvis' fifth record, 'Mystery Train', backed with 'I Forgot To Remember To Forget'. It is perhaps appropriate that this disc – which is to be his last for Sun – is a tune co-written by Sam Phillips and a black blues singer named Little Junior Parker. By now the success of Elvis' records are beginning to interest the major record companies, and Sam Phillips receives substantial offers for his contract from Columbia and Atlantic Records. Increasingly, Colonel Parker is becoming involved in negotiations, for he senses that, with aggressive promotion and recording with a major label, Elvis can be a huge star. 'I discovered the big secret that would send Elvis to the pinnacle of success,' he says rather enigmatically. 'Female entertainers have been using it for years to turn audiences on. I just had Elvis do it in reverse.' On this day, the Colonel signs an agreement with Elvis and Bob Neal to act as 'special adviser' to them both.

October 11, 1955. Start of a new tour in which Elvis is no longer part of a group of artists, but the *star!* 'The Elvis Presley Jamboree' kicks off in Texas, crosses the state and goes through Arkansas before winding up in St Louis. Two of the artists supporting Elvis are themselves destined for stardom: pianist Floyd Cramer and singer Johnny Cash who also records with Sun. While he is on the road, Elvis has also moved his parents into a new bungalow home at 1414 Getwell Road in Memphis.

November 2, 1955. 'Mystery Train' reaches the number one spot in the Country Charts – Elvis' first number one record and his biggest Sun record. This achievement coincides with the annual Disc Jockeys' Convention in Nashville where the assembled music men also vote him 'Most Promising New Singer'. Behind the scenes Colonel Parker is making the final arrangements to move Elvis to a new record label.

November 21, 1955. After intense competition among several labels to land Elvis, he signs for RCA Victor in a deal worth $35,000, worked out by the Colonel and RCA's man in Nashville, Steve Sholes. All the tapes Elvis has recorded for Sun are taken over by RCA, although Sam Phillips has a further year to merchandise his existing records. Elvis himself later recalls this important landmark in his career: 'It seems Mr Steve Sholes of the RCA Victor's specialties department had heard my first record, "That's All Right, Mama", and he asked around and recognised me. He went to Sun Records, who still had me signed to that first contract, and, well, they got to the Colonel and me and we talked it over. That's how I came to sign with RCA Victor.' Although the figure quoted may not seem large today, it is an unprecedented sum in 1955 for a new artist who has still to break into the nationwide pop music charts.

1956

January 10, 1956. After spending Christmas and the New Year at home with his parents, Elvis celebrates his 21st birthday and makes his first recordings for RCA at their studios in Nashville. In the label's rather primitive studios

Radio reporters and journalists become almost as persistent as the fans – but Elvis takes it in his stride.

at 1525 Mc Gavock Street, part of a building owned by the Methodist TV, Radio and Film Commission, he cuts five tunes in a three-hour session including 'I Got A Woman', 'Money Honey' and the new blues number which is to make him world famous, 'Heartbreak Hotel', written by publicist Mae Axton and songwriter Tommy Durden. In charge of the session is Chet Atkins, a skilful guitar player, who not only features on the five tunes with Elvis, Scotty, Bill, D.J. Fontana, piano player Floyd Cramer and vocalists, The Jordanaires, but exerts a tremendous influence on the creation of the sound which will turn Elvis from a success in the American South to an international phenomenon. (See special feature by Atkins.) Despite the historical importance of this session, the members of The Jordanaires, who have recorded with many top artists before, are not overly impressed. Leader Gordon Stoker says later, 'After the session, Elvis said if any of the songs went big, he wanted us to record all his stuff with him. We didn't think they'd

go big. We didn't think much about it at all. We didn't even remember Elvis' name, really. It was just another job for us.'

January 28, 1956. Elvis returns to New York, the city that had previously rejected him for television, to appear on the half-hour Tommy and Jimmy Dorsey 'Stage Show' produced by Jackie Gleason for CBS. The show is televised opposite the enormously popular 'Perry Como Show' and Elvis has been picked by executive producer Jack Philbin because 'he looks like a guitar-playing Marlon Brando' and should appeal to younger viewers. Elvis sings 'Blue Suede Shoes' and the not-yet-released 'Heartbreak Hotel' and brings an absolute deluge of mail to the show – as well as attacks on his 'lewd movements' from certain of the TV critics. Elvis makes six appearances on this show, on February 4, 11 and 18, and on March 17 and 24. The release of 'Heartbreak Hotel' is ideally timed for, as *Billboard* notes, 'Presley is riding high right now with network TV appearances and the disc should benefit from all the special plugging.' While in New York, Elvis also records for two

Steve Sholes, RCA's man in Nashville, signs Elvis to the label – though as the early advertisement (*below*) shows, he is billed as a straight Country & Western singer!

days at the RCA Studios on East 24th Street, and among the tunes are 'Blue Suede Shoes', 'Tutti Frutti' and 'Shake, Rattle and Roll'.

March 15, 1956. Bob Neal's contract as Elvis' manager expires and Colonel Tom Parker takes over the total running of his career. Neal, like Sam Phillips, accepts losing

the young man with good grace; both appreciating that he is destined for stardom and needs far more skilful handling than they can offer. Both have retained a place in the legend, nonetheless.

March 24, 1956. 'Heartbreak Hotel' reaches number one spot on the *Billboard* Country and Western Chart, and within a week is also top of the Rhythm and Blues and Pop Charts – the first ever record to achieve such a grand slam. Elvis, though, has scarcely a moment to enjoy his triumph, with a punishing series of appearances across the country; indeed in Jacksonville, Florida, he collapses, and although he is told to stay in hospital for a week, refuses and carries on with his engagements without a break. Says Scotty Moore, 'But we didn't know what was going on. We were working nearly every day. We never saw any newspapers. All we knew was drive, drive, drive.'

April 1, 1956. Elvis flies to Hollywood at the invitation of famous film-maker Hal Wallis to take a screen test. Wallis has approached Colonel Parker after seeing Elvis on one of the Dorsey television shows and coming to appreciate the impact he is having on audiences across America. Elvis is delighted, for, as he says later, 'Singers come and go – but if you're a good actor you can last a long time.' For his test, Elvis plays a scene from *The Rainmaker* opposite veteran actor, Frank Faylen. Of this now famous test at Paramount Pictures studios, Hal Wallis says, 'I felt the same thrill I experienced when I first saw Errol Flynn on the screen. Elvis, in a very different, modern way, had exactly the same power, virility and sexual drive. The camera caressed him.' The Colonel promptly draws up a seven-year contract for three films, the first for $100,000, and the fee for each

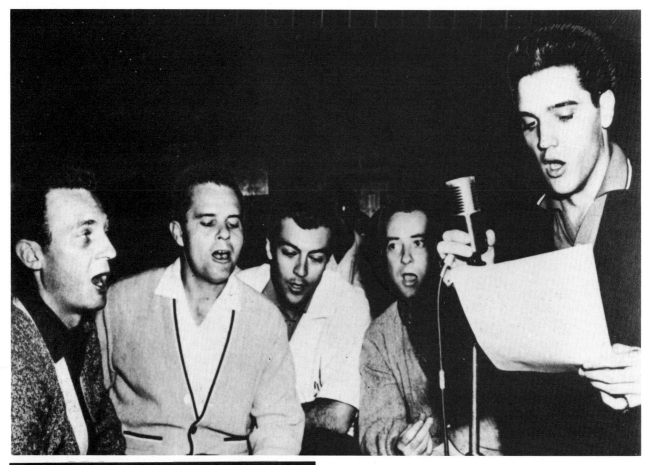

(*Above*) Elvis recording with The Jordanaires who were to cut a great many tunes with him over the years.

(*Left*) Rare still of Elvis' first major television appearance on the Dorsey Brothers' 'Stage Show' in early 1956.

subsequent one increased by $50,000. At the same time, he buys Elvis out of his contract with the 'Louisiana Hayride' where he has made 84 appearances. To terminate this arrangement, which still has to run until September, costs $10,000 and the agreement to play a grand 'farewell' concert – which eventually takes place at the Louisiana Fair Grounds on December 16, attended by 9,000 people.

April 3, 1956. While in Los Angeles, Elvis appears on the prestigious Milton Berle Show and his incredible rise to stardom is underlined when the show's ratings are revealed. The audience is estimated at 40 million, or one out of every four people in America. Because of this success, Elvis is booked for another show with Berle on June 5.

April 23, 1956. Elvis makes his debut in Las Vegas – the gambling city with which he is to become inextricably associated during the later part of his career. For a staggering fee of $12,500 per week, he plays the Venus Room night club of the New Frontier Hotel, with comedian Shecky Greene and the Freddie Martin Orchestra. But the shows are not a success – mainly because the audiences are

the Boundless Future
MOVIES SIGN ELVIS

Elvis knew his lines. Didn't miss a single cue

As screen test was shown, Wallis knew he had a star

Singer, dancer—no matter, this boy can act too!

Veteran Frank Faylen stands in amazement as Elvis exits

More rare pictures of Elvis making his screen test for Hal Wallis in Hollywood in April 1956.

Elvis stands proudly outside the new home he has bought his mother and father in Audubon Drive, Memphis in May 1956.

much older than those who usually come to see Elvis – and his engagement closes on April 29.

April 30, 1956. America's two top magazines, *Life* and *Time*, feature Elvis, 'the howling Hillbilly success' who overnight has become the biggest singing attraction for American teenagers. They report he has just bought two more Cadillacs and a new, ranch-style house at 1034, Audubon Drive, in one of the fashionable districts of Memphis. Commenting on their live appearances, D.J. Fontana says, 'From then on it became a battle. Hard to get into auditoriums and hard to get out. Sometimes we had to go in two or three hours ahead of time to avoid the crowds and then have a police car or something to get us out!'

June 5, 1956. Elvis makes a second appearance on the Milton Berle Show and unleashes a storm of protest about his singing and wiggling. Says Jack Gould of the *New York Times*, 'His one speciality is an accented movement of the body that heretofore has been primarily identified with the repertoire of the blonde bombshells of the burlesque runway. The gyration never had anything to do with the

world of popular music and still doesn't.' Jack O'Brien of the *New York Journal-American* goes even further: 'He can't sing a lick and makes up for his vocal shortcomings with the weirdest and plainly planned, suggestive animation short of an aborigine's mating dance.' And evangelist Billy Graham sums up the feelings of churchmen and women all over the country when he declares, 'I wouldn't let my daughter walk across the street to see Elvis Presley perform.' There are even those who think Elvis is 'demoralising the youth of America', and perhaps the most vociferous of his opponents is columnist Hedda Hopper who says that he is 'the most obscene and vulgar influence on young America today!'

Stung into a reply because he is worried about what his mother and father might think of all these attacks, Elvis says, 'I trust the Colonel – he is really like a daddy to me when I'm away from home. He had to make me controversial to get me going. But we haven't done anything bad.'

July 1, 1956. Another astonishing television appearance for Elvis in 'The Steve Allen Show' from New York. He performs a comedy skit with the host of the show, entitled 'Tumbleweed Presley', and sings 'Hound Dog' to a real Basset. Comments Steve Allen: 'We'd recognised the controversy that was building around Elvis and so we took advantage of it, putting him in a tuxedo – white tie and tails – and taking away his guitar. We thought putting Elvis in formal wardrobe to sing the song was humorous. We also asked him to stand perfectly still, and we positioned a real hound dog on a stool next to him – a dog that had been trained to do nothing but sit and look droopy. I must say Elvis took it quite naturally, and goodnaturedly.' Elvis is not, however, quite so goodnatured about the nickname which was now being used ever more frequently about him – Elvis the Pelvis. In an interview with *TV Guide* he says, 'I don't like being called Elvis the Pelvis. I mean, it's one of the most childish expressions I ever heard. But if they want to call me that, there ain't nothing I can do about it, so I have to accept it.'

July 2, 1956. Elvis records three more tunes in a second session at the RCA Studios in New York. It is to prove his last recording date in the city, although one of the songs, 'Hound Dog', proves his biggest hit single of the fifties, selling more than 5,000,000 copies within a year. According to reports, Elvis is not keen to record 'Hound Dog', although it is a favourite at his concerts. Steve Sholes makes him change his mind, but 31 takes are required before a satisfactory version is completed!

July 4, 1956. 'The Elvis Presley Show' takes to the road for a summer of one-night stands which are later described as 'the dizzy apogee of his career as a rock star.' The frantic pace makes Elvis burn with nervous excitement, as Scotty Moore and the others later remember. 'He had so much nervous energy he was always talking and clowning,' says Scotty. 'We'd sometimes have to wear him out so we could go to sleep. Every day, every night it was the same.' On this

A highlight from Elvis' appearance on the Steve Allen Show on July 1 1956 – the sketch 'Tumbleweed Presley'.

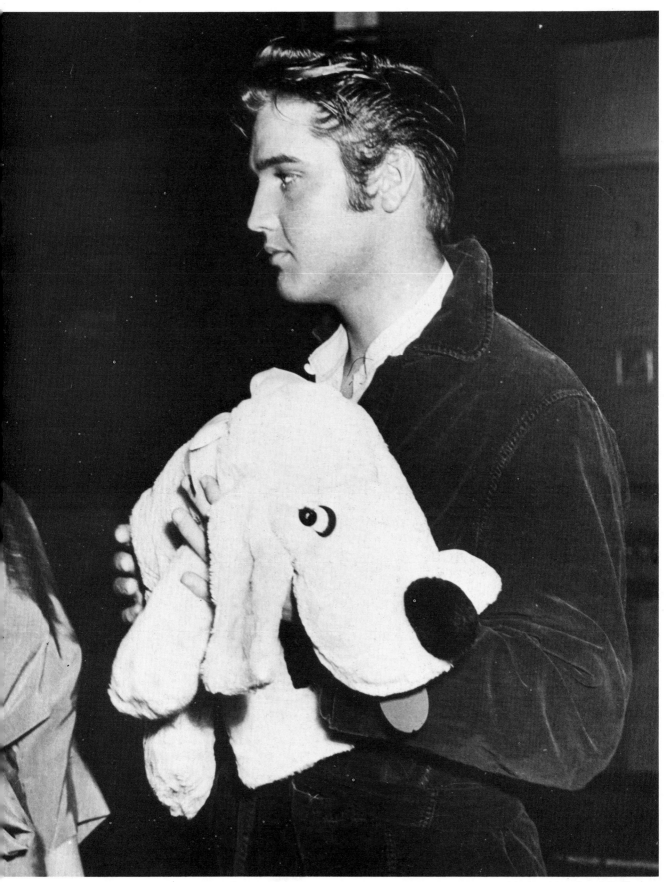

Elvis meeting his co-stars in his first film, *Love Me Tender*,
Richard Egan and Debra Paget.

'Elvis Presley Day' in Tupelo: the star and his parents
return to their home town in triumph in September 1956.

date Elvis gives a big charity benefit show at the Russwood
Stadium in Memphis. He faces his biggest ever live
audience – 14,000 people – and tells his cheering hometown
fans, 'I just want to say to you all not to worry – those
people in New York and Hollywood are not gonna change
me *none*!

July 25, 1956. Speculation is rife in the press about Elvis'
projected first film to begin shooting in August. Although it
is known several ideas have been discussed by Hal Wallis
at Paramount – including a musical, *The Pied Piper of
Cleveland* – Elvis is instead loaned to 20th Century Fox to
appear in a Western provisionally titled, *The Reno Brothers*.

August 22, 1956. Elvis begins work in Hollywood on *The
Reno Brothers* which is quickly revised to cash in on his
popularity as a singer by the introduction of four songs, one
of which, 'Love Me Tender', is chosen to be the final title of
the film. Co-starring with Elvis are Richard Egan and
Debra Paget. The director is Robert D. Webb, and the
producer David Weisbart who had produced James Dean's
famous movie, *Rebel Without A Cause*, the previous year; and

so the press has a field day drawing comparisons between
the two teenage idols. Weisbart himself comments, 'So far
as teenagers are concerned, Elvis is what I call a safety
valve. By that I mean they scream, holler, articulate, and
let go of their emotions when they see him perform. But
when they watched Jimmy perform they bottled their
emotions and were sort of sullen and brooding. Elvis is
completely outgoing, whereas Jimmy was the direct
opposite. Basically, Jimmy was a loner, whereas Elvis is
gregarious.' Despite this difference, Weisbart discusses with
Elvis the possibility of starring him in *The Jimmy Dean Story*,
based on the life of the young rebel who had died the
previous year. Although Elvis is delighted at the very idea,
the picture, sadly, is never made.

September 9, 1956. The extent of Elvis' phenomenal rise to
fame is demonstrated when 54 million people – 82.6 per
cent of the television viewing public of America – tune in
to watch his appearance on Ed Sullivan's Sunday night
'Toast of the Town' show. Elvis records his segment for the
programme at the CBS Studios in Hollywood, but his host
Ed Sullivan is unable to see the young star he has paid
$50,000 for three appearances, as he has been injured in a
car accident, and standing in his place in New York where
the 'live' part of the show goes out is veteran actor, Charles
Laughton. Although Sullivan misses this record-breaking

42

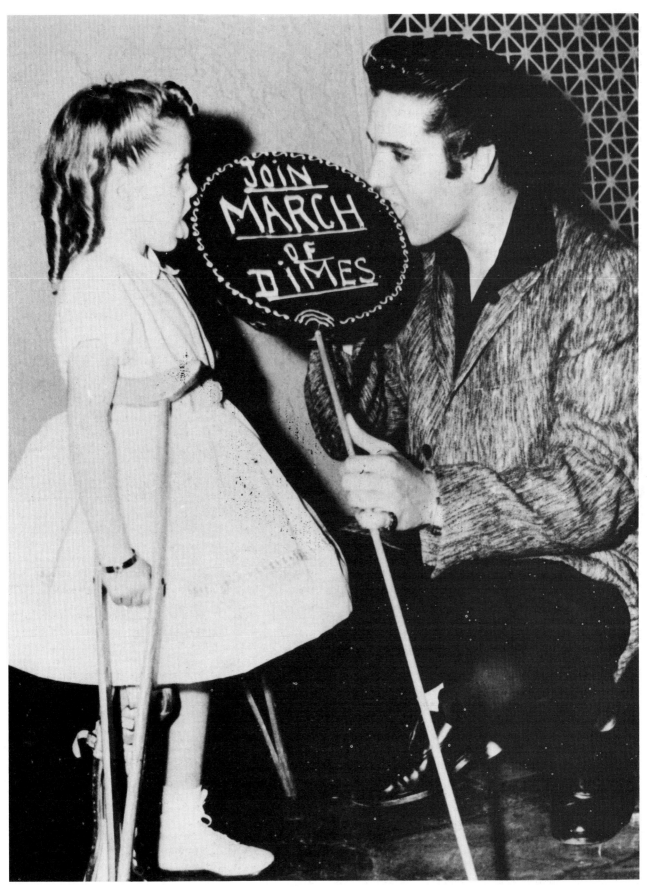

Elvis helping in the 'March of Dimes' campaign in 1957.

The 'Million Dollar Quartet' in action in December 1956 watched by an admiring Marion Keisker. From left to right, Jerry Lee Lewis, Carl Perkins, Elvis and Johnny Cash.

performance (the viewing figures are to remain unchallenged until 1964 when the Beatles appear on the self-same show), he is the host when Elvis returns on October 28 and again on January 6, just before his birthday. It is on the *final* performance, incidentally, that he is televised from the waist upwards – not the first as generally believed – because of the massive media and public reaction against his 'sexual cavortings'.

September 26, 1956. This is declared 'Elvis Presley Day' when Elvis returns to his birthplace, Tupelo, to perform at the Mississippi-Alabama Fair and Dairy Show where he had first performed in public. He donates $10,000 to the establishment of a youth centre and park around the area where he was born, which is eventually to be known as the 'Elvis Presley Foundation For Under-Privileged Children'. Elvis, who is accompanied by his mother and father, is also given a three-foot long guitar-shaped 'Key' to the town by Mayor Jim Ballard who says, 'This town's proud to call you its son.'

October 1, 1956. A Chicago radio station, WAIT, plays tunes by Elvis for twelve hours uninterrupted – 133 in all – and the following day is swamped by requests to repeat the same thing *every day*. Such events, though, are condemned by the media as 'pandering to the worst juvenile tastes' and

causing teenage riots. According to *New York Daily News*, these riots are taking place 'from puritanical Boston to julep-loving Georgia' and the paper demands a crack-down on 'riotous rock 'n' roll', with all teenagers banned from dancing in public without the written consent of their parents!

October 19, 1956. The Hollywood trade papers carry the announcement that Elvis Presley's next film is to be *Lonesome Cowboy,* co-starring 'bare-all actress, Jayne Mansfield'. RCA also begin to promote Elvis' records in the European market with references to another sex symbol. 'He walks like Marilyn Monroe,' says the trailer, 'but at home he's a model son!'

October 23, 1956. In a three-part newspaper series syndicated across America, Colonel Parker is quoted as saying that he now wants 'hustlers not publicity now Elvis is a big show business name.' Interviewed by William Steif in 'What Makes Elvis Tick?', the Colonel explains that with 'Elvis on top of the heap, the main chance is for merchandisers to make a lot of money through Presley licences. That's why hustlers are needed.' This is to start an avalanche of products bearing Elvis' likeness which have continued unabated to this day. Steif concludes his series by calling Elvis 'a God-loving, jelly-kneed kid who's taken rock 'n' roll out of the category of race or rhythm-and-blues music and made it into pops.'

October 24, 1956. Variety headlines its issue 'Elvis A

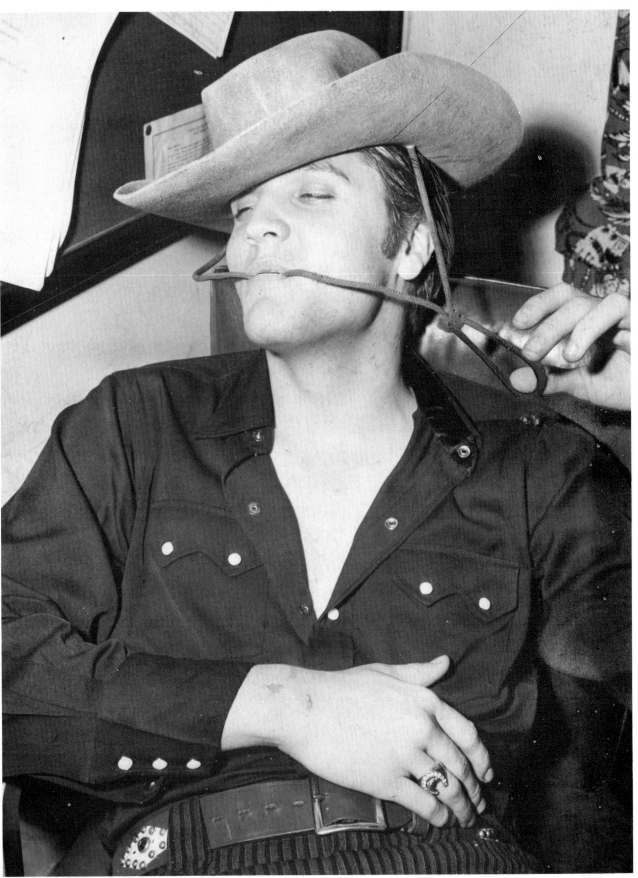

A far from 'Lonesome Cowboy' in February 1957.

'The King of Rock 'n' Roll' in his famous gold lamé tuxedo in August 1957.

Millionaire in One Year' and declares the young singer to be 'the King of Rock 'n' Roll', having risen from an obscure country singer playing small dates in the South to a 'door-busting crowd puller and chart topper' in less than twelve months. Adds reporter Mike Kaplan, 'Controversy has always meant cash in show business and the latest proof is Elvis Presley, whose jet-propelled career will reach strato-spheric heights in his first full year in the bigtime with an indicated gross income of at least $1,000,000. Tally is an underestimation, based on what he has done in the first nine months of 1956.' Advance orders for his record of 'Love Me Tender' are said to be almost one million, according to the paper.

This same day, English readers of the *Sunday Express* get the first detailed account of the Presley phenomenon by one of the few reporters able to interview Elvis before the Colonel's publicity close-down, Peter Dacre. (Mr Dacre recalls his incredible meeting with a legend in this book.)

November 16, 1956. Love Me Tender opens in New York to

generally poor reviews but an ecstatic reception from the fans who line the streets to gain admission to the Paramount Theatre. Within three weeks, the picture has recouped its costs of one million dollars, and this return on investment is to stand as a record until the advent of *Star Wars* and the other Science Fiction films of the 1980s.

December 4, 1956. Elvis returns to Memphis to spend Christmas with his family, and perhaps not surprisingly drops by Sun Records on Union Avenue to see Sam Phillips. There he finds three other artists, his friend Johnny Cash, Carl Perkins and Jerry Lee Lewis, in attendance, and for almost two hours they all talk and occasionally sing together. A reporter from the *Memphis Press-Scimitar*, tipped off as to what is happening, later writes: 'Elvis headed for the piano and started to play "Blueberry Hill". The joint was really rocking before they got through. That quartet could sell a million!' Among the tunes the four men sing and play are 'Island of Golden Dreams', 'I Won't Have To Cross Jordan Alone', 'The Old Rugged Cross' and 'Down By The Riverside', and as a result of the reporter's comment the assembly becomes known as 'The Million Dollar Quartet'. A record of this amazing quartet is later released in London in 1980.

December 22, 1956. To pay tribute to WIDA, the Memphis r & b radio station to which he had listened as a youngster and which had influenced his music, Elvis plays a benefit concert in company with Little Junior Parker, co-writer of one of his earliest recordings, 'Mystery Train', and the famous blues singer, B.B. King.

1957

January 4, 1957. Just before his twenty-second birthday, Elvis reports to the Kennedy Veterans Hospital in Memphis to take the traditional medical check-up required of all young American men who might be called up to the Armed Services. The Chairman of the Draft Board, Captain E. P. Rowan, declares that Elvis is 'an A-profile and that's as high as you can go', but that he has no idea when he might be drafted. The press are there in force to cover the medical, and there are several scuffles when more persistent photographers try to get shots of Elvis, naked, undergoing medical examination. There is also the beginning of much speculation as to whether Elvis will be called up and, if he is, whether he will be given an 'easy number' as an entertainer for the troops or used as part of a publicity recruiting campaign.

January 12, 1957. Elvis goes to Hollywood to spend two days with Scotty, Bill, D.J. and The Jordanaires at Radio Recorders studio and, apart from a group of outstanding religious songs, he also cuts 'All Shook Up', his next single release which is to prove his greatest chart success, remaining at the number one spot for an unprecedented *eight weeks*!

January 20, 1957. Work begins on Elvis' second movie,

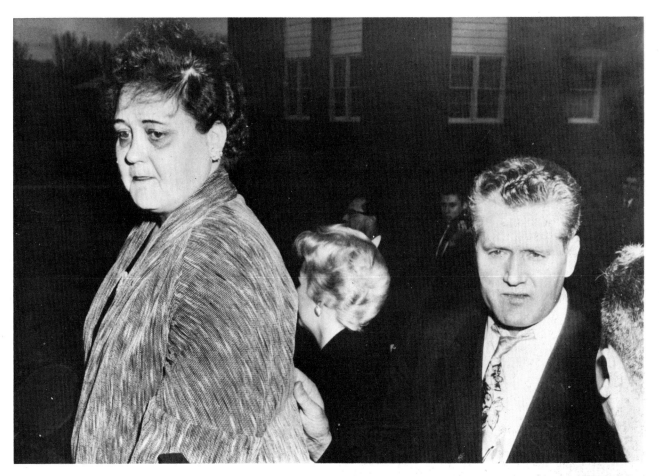

A visibly upset Gladys and Vernon Presley (*above*) see their boy off to do his Army service on March 24 1958. Elvis has to run the usual gauntlet of fans and press photographers before he can settle down to being a soldier. (*below*).

A somewhat rueful looking Elvis during his early days as a
soldier!

Certainly not blue suede shoes – but very useful on the
long hikes Elvis has to take with his platoon.

A little off-duty pleasure for Elvis meeting some of the
stars of the Frankfurt Ice Show.

Loving You, his first for Hal Wallis, the producer who had screen-tested him. Cast as Deke Rivers in Hal Kanter's story, Elvis plays a figure very much like himself who rises from being a truck driver to singing stardom. Lizabeth Scott and Dolores Hart provide the female interest, and there is an interesting moment during one of Elvis' theatre performances when his mother and father – who had made the trip to Hollywood with him – are seen among the cheering audience. Again the picture is changed from its original title of *Lonesome Cowboy*, but the projected appearance of Jayne Mansfield fails to materialise.

March 19, 1957. Because of the constant attention of fans around the Presley home on Audubon Drive (which has brought complaints from neighbours as well as considerable inconvenience to Gladys and Vernon), Elvis buys Graceland, an imposing 1910 mansion with its white-columned portico entrance, in the exclusive Memphis suburb of Whitehaven. Empty for some years and only occasionally used as a Sunday School, it offers extensive grounds and the opportunity to be modelled in exactly the way the family require. Elvis pays $102,500 for Graceland and comments, 'It will be a lot nicer than any film star's house when I get it the way I want it.' This is to be his home for the rest of his life.

May 1, 1957. Jailhouse Rock, Elvis' third film, is shot with breathtaking speed by director Richard Thorpe for MGM. As a prisoner who has accidentally killed a man, Elvis is turned into a singing star by a cell-mate, only to fall prey to the temptations of show business before being rescued by the love of Judy Tyler. Highlights of the film are the four songs – including the title tune – written by the superb Jerry Leiber and Mike Stoller partnership. Elvis, with his usual musicians and The Jordanaires, also goes into the MGM recording studios in Culver City to cut these and three other tracks for a special LP to be released with the film.

June 6, 1957. Release of the film *Loving You*, plus a single featuring the title song and backed with 'Teddy Bear' written by Kal Mann and Bernie Lowe. The tune has been written – its authors say – because of Elvis' fondness for these soft toys and his unerring ability to win them on amusement sideshows. The record brings a deluge of teddy bear gifts from fans to Graceland – then in the process of being renovated – as well as giving rise to a line of 'Elvis Presley Teddy Bears' which appear in shops all over America. The tune itself occupies the number one spot in the charts through much of July and August.

August 28, 1957. After a vacation – his first break in two years – Elvis undertakes his first tour of the Pacific Northwest. This three-week jamboree is also to prove his last concert tour until the 1970s. As the unchallenged 'King of Rock 'n' Roll', he now has a costume to match the part – a $10,000 gold lamé tuxedo made by the Hollywood costume firm of Nudie's. Although stunningly effective on stage, this famous suit proves very hot and cumbersome

when worn, and Elvis eventually discards it. The tour is a fabulous success, grossing $147,000 for five half-hour performances. The biggest date proves to be Vancouver on September 1, where the box office takes $44,000, but such is the hysteria of fans trying to get near Elvis that he has to flee from the stage before the end of his act. Comments Gordon Stoker of The Jordanaires, 'I can't express that experience, being on stage with as many as thirty thousand people screaming and hollering. Elvis didn't seem to understand the audience reaction to him and so he'd have fun, he'd put them on. He always wanted us in as close to him as possible. Scotty and Bill, too. He wanted the protection. The girls were at fever pitch by the time he got through. At one concert they were begging for something he owned and he threw his coat into the audience. It was like throwing a pound of meat to a pack of hungry dogs. They tore it to shreds.'

October 28, 1957. Elvis climaxes his touring at the Pan-Pacific Auditorium in Los Angeles, attracting a capacity crowd of 9,200 people on each of two evenings and taking $56,000. Because of complaints in certain sections of the media that his first performance is 'obscene', Elvis tells his audience on the second night: 'I'm sorry this came up, but we're not going to let it stop us from putting on the best show we can for you people. If they think it's obscene, that's their problem, not mine.' This tour also marks the parting of the ways for Elvis with Scotty and Bill who have seen him rise from obscurity to an international celebrity. Though they will record with him in the future, they never travel on the road again. 'Like any group that lives together you build up to these things, so Bill and I quit,' says Scotty. 'Elvis wasn't doing much touring anyway, and he could just call us for recordings. We just booked it by the day. We'd just hire on, and then go and do something else until he needed us again.'

December 20, 1957. On his return to Graceland for Christmas, Chairman of the Memphis Draft Board Milton Bowers delivers to Elvis in person the news that he is to be drafted. An album of favourite Christmas tunes which Elvis had recorded in September, 'Elvis' Christmas Album', tops the charts, although hopes that it will appeal to adults as well as youngsters are dashed when a large number of radio stations inexplicably refuse to play the LP, claiming it is in 'bad taste'.

1958

January 20, 1958. Elvis reports at the Memphis Draft Board and is declared 1A. He tells the assembled horde of pressmen, 'It's a duty I've got to fill and I'm going to do it. I'm kinda proud of it.' Despite the Navy having offered Elvis his own company made up of Memphis boys to enlist with them, it is for the Army he is destined – after a sixty-day deferment which is granted because of his contracted film for Paramount, *King Creole*.

January 23, 1958. To film in Hollywood, Elvis travels by

Home again! America welcomes Elvis in March 1960.

train and, believing it will be the last time they will see him for two years while he is in the Army, thousands of fans gather beside the railway tracks. 'No matter what time of day or night,' says one report, 'people were lined along the tracks all the way across America.' The story of *King Creole*, in which Elvis features as a young boy battling the seamy underworld of New Orleans, requires studio work in Hollywood and – for the first time in his career – location work in the famous old Southern city. The main problems for producer Hal Wallis and director Michael Curtiz are to keep the fans at bay while filming in the French Quarter. While in Hollywood, Elvis records the musical numbers for the film, and on February 1 cuts a new single, 'Wear My Ring Around Your Neck', obviously intended as a 'farewell' for his fans as he is called up: but it is not released until 1965.

March 24, 1958. At 6.30 am – half an hour early – Elvis arrives at Local Board 86 in Memphis to begin Army life. Although Elvis has allowed photographers into Graceland the previous evening, dozens are waiting to picture his induction, as well as hundreds of fans and Colonel Tom Parker handing out balloons advertising *King Creole*! After a medical at Kennedy Hospital, he is sworn in, given his Army number of US53310761, and swops his monthly pay-packet of over $100,000 for just $78. Says Elvis, 'I am looking forward to it as a great experience. If they make it tough for me, it won't be due to anything I do. The Army can do anything it wants with me. Millions of other guys have been drafted, and I don't want to be different from anyone else.' The coverage of Elvis entering the Army continues until he is safely installed at Fort Chaffee in Arkansas, which he leaves a few days later to be based at Fort Hood in Texas. Here he is assigned to A Company of the Second Medium Tank Battalion, the famed 'Hell on Wheels' Division.

June 10, 1958. Having completed his first spell of training, Elvis is given two weeks' leave from the Army. During this time, he returns to Memphis for a premiere of *King Creole* (which he thoroughly enjoys: it is to remain his favourite film) and also goes to Nashville to cut five tunes in the RCA Studios. Only D. J. Fontana of his original group is present among the group of session men, lead by Chet Atkins, although the vocals are once more provided by The Jordanaires. The five songs are all to prove smash hits – 'I Need Your Love Tonight', 'A Big Hunk O'Love', 'Ain't That Loving You Baby', 'A Fool Such As I' and 'I Got Stung'. On his return to Fort Hood, Elvis installs his mother and father in a nearby house at 609 Oak Hill Drive, Killeen. He also learns that in September he is to be sent to Germany.

August 8, 1958. Because of a marked decline in Gladys Presley's health, Elvis sends her back to Memphis to see her own specialists. Her illness is diagnosed as hepatitis and she is moved into a private room at the Methodist Hospital. Three days later, Elvis receives an urgent telephone call at Fort Hood to return home.

Was it just a bad dream? Elvis seems to be wondering as he leaves the Army!

August 14, 1958. After seeming to rally with Elvis at her bedside, Gladys Presley dies. She is just 46 and her death is diagnosed as a heart attack. Four hundred guests are invited to the funeral, but thousands of fans stand mourning outside Graceland. Gladys is buried in Forest Hills Cemetery, three miles outside Memphis, beneath an inscription which reads: 'Beloved wife of Vernon Presley and mother of Elvis Presley – She was the Sunshine of our Home'. Later the grief-stricken Elvis says of his mother, 'She was very close, more than a mother. She was a friend who would let me talk to her any hour of the day or night if I had a problem. I would get mad sometimes when she wouldn't let me do something. But I found out she was right about almost everything.' Elvis is given an extended leave by the Army, and when he returns to Fort Hood on August 24, he says he is keeping a promise to his mother that he and his father will never be separated. Vernon Presley is to accompany him to Europe when he is posted.

September 19, 1958. His training completed, Elvis travels by train across America to the Military Ocean Terminal in Brooklyn to sail to Germany. With 1,300 other soldiers, he leaves America for the first time in his life on September

22, aboard the *USS General Randall*. His press conference is recorded by RCA and later released as an EP, 'Elvis Sails'. In response to a question about what he'd most like to see in Europe, he replies, 'Paris – and I'd like to look up Brigitte Bardot.' Does he think his popularity has declined through being in the Army? 'No. I'd say my fan mail has doubled – around 15,000 letters a week – and it's been driving them crazy down at Fort Hood!' He's enjoying Army life, he adds, and none of the fellows have been rough on him – though some have given him unprintable nicknames!

September 29, 1958. During the sea voyage to Germany, Elvis helps stage a concert on board the *USS General Randall*. He produces and directs the show, singing three numbers himself, and earns a standing ovation from the soldiers and crew. As the ship is sailing down the English Channel, it is halted to take on a pilot, and Elvis stands for some while staring at the famous white cliffs of Dover. This is to prove the nearest he ever comes to England during his lifetime.

October 1, 1958. Five hundred German fans, and walls daubed with the message, 'Elvis über alles!' greet the singer-turned-soldier when he docks at Bremerhaven – but the crowds only catch a fleeting glimpse of their hero as a train takes him to the Army base at Friedburg, just north of Frankfurt, where he is to be stationed for the next seventeen months. Pressmen and photographers again have access to Elvis until October 5 when the post becomes off-limits to all civilians.

November 20, 1958. Elvis is transferred from being a tank crew member to a scout jeep driver, a better status assignment for a soldier already proving himself above normal capability. His battalion also goes to Grafenwohr for training with other West German and US troops. A feature of the training here is handling all kinds of weapons from pistols to 90mm guns, and Elvis proves himself an adept pupil.

November 26, 1958. Another recognition of Elvis' ability as a soldier when he is made a Private First Class on Thanksgiving – his salary entering the three figure bracket at $100 per month. A citation from his battalion reads, 'We hope nobody complains that Elvis was promoted before other soldiers in his unit, but he really tries hard to be a good soldier and he deserves it.' Elvis himself comments, 'I'm proud to have a stripe,' and rewards himself by purchasing a white $7,160 BMW sports car upholstered in white leather, to drive to and from the camp each day.

1959

January 8, 1959. To mark Elvis' birthday, Dick Clark dedicates his popular 'American Bandstand' television programme to him and rings him in Germany. Over live television, he tells Elvis that he has been voted 'Best Singer of the Year' in the US and 'King Creole' the 'Best Record of the Year'. Viewers listen fascinated to his description of life in the Army in Europe. He also reveals that he has

found a house for his father at Goethestrasse 14 in Bad Nauheim, and will live with him there when not carrying out Army duties. He also dispels a rumour that has been fanned by German reporters that he has actually been looking for a castle or at least a mediaeval mansion in which to live!

January 15, 1959. Hearts miss a beat when a Frankfurt newspaper publishes an unconfirmed report that Elvis has died in a car crash! According to the story, a white BMW has been wrecked in a terrible accident and there are fears the horribly mutilated driver might be Elvis. The telephones at the base ring red-hot as the world's press seek confirmation of the story, and a public relations officer goes almost hoarse repeating the official statement: 'Elvis Presley is alive, well, and happy, and was not involved in any accident.' To dispel the lingering rumour and show just how well and healthy he is, Elvis gives blood to the German Red Cross two days later!

February 2, 1959. Although Elvis generally spends his off-duty hours with his father and friends, he emerges daily to sign autographs for fans waiting in Goethestrasse. He also occasionally visits local shows, and on this day is photographed at the Frankfurt Ice Show posing with some of the stars.

May, 1959. Elvis develops an interest in Karate as a result of being introduced to one of Germany's leading instructors, Jurgen Seydel. For a while Elvis is able to train at Seydel's studio in Usingen, but when persistent fans threaten to disrupt the proceedings, these are continued at the Presley house in Goethestrasse. The interest in Karate is to last for much of the rest of Elvis' life.

June 14, 1959. Elvis is promoted again – this time to Specialist Fourth Class, the technical equivalent of a Corporal, and his pay rises to $122 per month! He comments, 'I'm doing OK in this man's Army – and take it from me, it's a rough, tough Army that could give anybody, anywhere, any time, one hell of a fight.' Tough words – but Elvis isn't tough enough to ward off an attack of tonsilitis and has to spend a week in bed in the Army's 97th General Hospital in Frankfurt. Afterwards he whispers, 'It was touch and go whether they'd snatch my cotton-pickin' tonsils, but my fever burned out.' Elvis is given a 14-day leave and visits Munich and then Paris where he has to face a press conference attended by more than 100 journalists. He even manages a brief stroll in the city streets before French fans spot him, and he has to restrict the rest of his stay to carefully planned visits, including one to the famous Lido.

September 18, 1959. The beautiful daughter of an American Air Force Captain stationed in Germany, 14-year-old Priscilla Beaulieu, is introduced to Elvis and he immediately falls for the delightful, dark-haired girl. They are to meet frequently during the rest of his tour of duty in Germany, and she is to follow him back to Graceland and, eventually,

Elvis was able to put the experience he gained as a tank crew member in the Army to good use in his first post-service film *G.I. Blues*.

Elvis with Frank Sinatra in his 'Welcome Elvis' TV
special in March 1960.

marry him. It was singularly appropriate that this month RCA should release a new album entitled 'A Date With Elvis'!

1960

January 8, 1960. Elvis throws a big party to celebrate his 25th birthday, with over 200 people attending. He is also promoted yet again, to Sergeant, and put in charge of a three-man reconnaissance team for the Third Armoured Division's 32nd Scout Platoon. As his last exercise in the Army, he takes part in a fourteen-day training run in the Black Forest called 'Operation Snowshield'.

March 1, 1960. The end of the Army career of Sergeant Presley, and as he prepares to fly home to America, the world's press speculates on what awaits the teenage idol after two years' absence. Elvis flies from Frankfurt to Fort Dix, New Jersey, making a brief stopover at Prestwick Airport in Scotland where, for what is to be the only time in his life, he stands on British soil for a few minutes.

March 5, 1960. Elvis is discharged from the Army, delightedly brandishing a Certificate of Achievement which cites his 'faithful duty and service'. He is met by Colonel Tom Parker and at a press conference announces that he 'probably won't grow my sideburns back'. He travels by train to Memphis, while a tribute to his Army career is placed in the Congressional Record by the Tennessee Senator, Estes Kefauver.

March 20, 1960. After a triumphant homecoming at

Demonstrating a 'moody sensitivity' in *Flaming Star*.

Elvis relaxing with a group of friends in the Memphis Fairgrounds Amusement Park.

Graceland, Elvis goes to RCA Studios in Nashville to cut a new single, and from the six tunes comes the timely, 'Soldier Boy' and 'Stuck On You' which is released two weeks later – with advance orders in excess of one million – and shoots straight up the charts. A national magazine, *The Post*, announces that it is to serialise a diary that Elvis kept of his time in the Army – paying $250,000 for the privilege. The Colonel responds: 'If such a diary had been written and such a sum been paid, we'd certainly have known about it, and we *don't!*'

March 26, 1960. Elvis reappears before his public as a whole when he stars in Frank Sinatra's 'Timex Special' show televised from The Fountainbleau Hotel in Miami, receiving the staggering fee of $125,000. He sings 'Stuck on You' and 'Fame and Fortune' and duets with Frank on two other tunes. The 'Welcome Elvis' special, as it is known, is seen by 41.5 per cent of the nation's viewers when it is aired on May 12.

April 26, 1960. Back to Hollywood to begin his first movie in over two years – the appropriate *GI Blues*, for which Hal Wallis had already shot some location footage while Elvis was still in the Army. Director Norman Taurog is soon talking to the press about Elvis playing a tank gunner

trying to break down the resistance of a night club dancer played by Juliet Prowse. 'He is a natural,' says Taurog. 'He is the most relaxed boy you could want. He reminds me of Crosby and Como. He is a good listener, and when you are a good listener you get to be a good actor.' Although the film is to be a box office success – grossing $4.3 million – it is not well received by the press when released in October.

July 3, 1960. Vernon Presley marries Dee Elliott, a lady he had met in Germany, at a private ceremony in Huntsville, Alabama. Elvis is not present.

August 8, 1960. The first straight acting role for Elvis in *Flaming Star*, playing the half-breed son of a Kiowa Indian and a white rancher in this 20th Century Fox film which takes forty-two days to shoot, a lot on location at the San Fernando Valley. He demonstrates a moody skill which pleases sections of the press and fascinates fans when the movie is released just before Christmas. While in Hollywood, Elvis records the title song and three other tunes for the picture.

November 7, 1960. Elvis makes his last picture for 20th Century Fox, *Wild In The Country*, in which he turns in a well-observed performance as a rather sullen and sexy young man who has to overcome violent tendencies and prejudice to make his way in the world. The original ending, with co-star Hope Lange committing suicide, is changed to allow Elvis to save her from carbon monoxide poisoning, and the pair also duet on the song 'Husky Dusky Day'. However, because of the comparative lack of success of this 'dramatic role' for Elvis, there are to be few such filming opportunities for him again.

December 4, 1960. In recognition of his 'constructive portrayal of a man of Indian blood in *Flaming Star*', Elvis is inducted into the Los Angeles Indian Tribal Council by Chief Wah-Nee-Ota. At the ceremony, Colonel Parker reveals that Elvis now has 5,000 fan clubs around the world and that his organisation alone is processing 30,000 fan letters a month! To mark this Christmas, Elvis records a selection of his favourite religious songs with The Jordanaires for what is to prove one of his most enduring albums, 'His Hand In Mine'.

1961

February 25, 1961. A red-letter day for local fans when Elvis appears in two benefit shows in Memphis at the Ellis Auditorium. The proceeds are to go to several local charities – including his own Under-Privileged Children's project – and both performances at the 5,500 seater venue are filled by ecstatic fans. With a nice acknowledgement to his past touring days, Elvis and his group close with 'Hound Dog' and Scotty Moore says afterwards, 'We never ever really tried to top that song. Elvis felt "Hound Dog" was the one they wanted and that was what he gave them. And they always reacted the same way – it just laid them out. It was a riot every time.'

A delightful moment from *Follow That Dream*, filming in 1961.

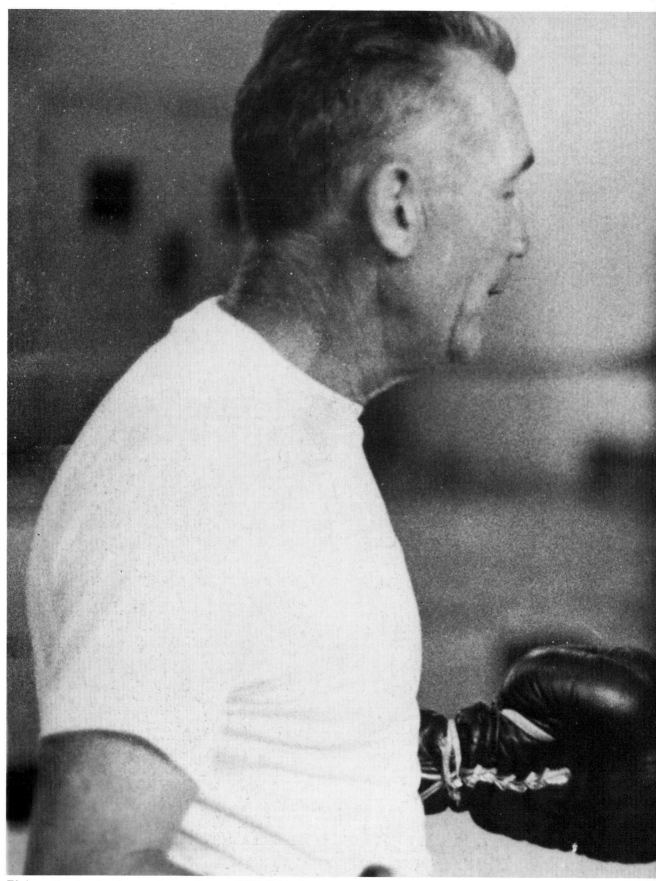

Elvis getting boxing instruction on the set of *Kid Galahad*.

Horse riding becomes another of Elvis' passions: he is pictured here riding in the grounds of Graceland.

March 8, 1961. At a meeting of the Tennessee State Legislature at Nashville, Elvis is given the title of an 'Honorary Colonel' (to match Colonel Tom's?) by the Governor of Tennessee, Buford Ellington. The legislators also pay tribute to him for bringing 'fame to Memphis and Tennessee' and for all his charitable work. Elvis tells the gathering, 'I can sincerely say that this is the finest honour I have ever received. And to people who are wondering if I plan to settle in Hollywood, let me say my home is in Memphis and that's where it's going to stay!'

March 25, 1961. A flight to beautiful Hawaii and a special benefit concert to raise money for the Memorial Fund of the *USS Arizona*, sunk by Japanese bombers during World War II. A crowd of 2,500 fans greet him at Honolulu, and over 4,000 pack the Bloch Arena in Pearl Harbour close to where the attack took place. In what is to be Elvis' last live performance until 1969, he sings nineteen songs – a record total for his shows – and raises $47,000 for the fund. He and the Colonel add another $5,000.

April 3, 1961. Staying on in Hawaii, Elvis shoots location footage for his next picture, *Blue Hawaii*, another Hal Wallis production for Paramount which co-stars him with Joan Blackman and Angela Lansbury. When released at Thanksgiving, it quickly grosses $4.7 million and finds a place on *Variety's* list of all-time box office successes. The later sound track album, 'Blue Hawaii', becomes the fastest selling LP of 1961 with total sales in excess of $5 million! This picture also becomes the prototype of the majority of Elvis' remaining films.

July 3, 1961. Elvis has a chance to play some nice comedy situations in *Follow That Dream* which reunites him with producer David Weisbart. Much of the picture is shot on location in Florida where Elvis is a member of a family of wandering hillbillies trying to outwit the local authorities' attempts to settle them down.

October 31, 1961. A busy year continues for Elvis as he begins work on a boxing story, *Kid Galahad*, which links him with film stars Gig Young and Charles Bronson. Because of his Karate expertise, Elvis makes his boxing scenes look very realistic, although some fans are reportedly concerned in case he might suffer real injury.

March 18, 1962. A night's work at the RCA Studios in Nashville produces an album and a single, before Elvis returns to Hollywood to film *Girls, Girls, Girls* for the old team of Hal Wallis and Norman Taurog. Despite the title and publicity photographs, there are only two main female roles in the picture, played by Stella Stevens and Laurel Goodwin. And although written by Edward Anhalt (an Oscar winner), with the title song composed by Jerry Leiber and Mike Stoller, and twelve more tunes, only the track 'Return To Sender' by Otis Blackwell is memorable – and indeed becomes a million seller.

May, 1962. Priscilla Beaulieu becomes a permanent resident at Graceland where, with the permission of her father, she continues her education at the Immaculate Conception High School in Memphis. Later she is to go to finishing school and study modelling and dancing. When Elvis returns to Memphis in between filming, he and Priscilla get great enjoyment horse riding together. Elvis is also still playing American football with groups of friends in Hollywood and Memphis (where he usually hires the local school field to play!).

November, 1962. In Hollywood once more, Elvis records the ten songs for his next picture, *It Happened At The World's Fair*, including 'One Broken Heart For Sale' which is to prove among his most disappointing singles in chart terms, reaching no higher than the number eleven spot, although its total sales eventually top the million mark. The MGM film stars Elvis as a pilot seeking to reclaim his impounded plane, who gets sidetracked by a lovely nurse, Joan O'Brien, and a waif-like Chinese child, Vicky Tiu.

1963

January 22, 1963. The year opens on a Mexican note for Elvis when he records eleven new songs for his next picture, *Fun in Acapulco*, and the musical accompanists in the Radio Recorders Studio in Hollywood are augmented by a vocal group, The Amigos. In Acapulco itself Elvis enjoys the beach location work, and the female company of Ursula Andress and Elsa Cardenas. In the film he's a trapeze artist who has lost his nerve and has to make a sudden plunge from a cliff-top – which naturally enough cures his fear.

May 26, 1963. Another of Elvis' increasingly rare returns to Nashville to cut songs for a new album unconnected with a film. In a two-day session he records 14 songs, from which 'Devil In Disguise' is picked as a single release and soars away to gold in record time.

August 4, 1963. Las Vegas, where Elvis is later to score such success in live concerts, is the setting for *Viva Las Vegas* in which he plays a racing driver, Lucky Jackson. He gets lucky in more ways than one – raising the money he needs for a new engine for his car and also winning the love of a night club dancer, played by Ann-Margaret. The couple

sing a duet on screen and the newspapers make much of an off-screen romance between the two – but nothing materialises. The picture, though, proves one of Elvis' most successful musicals, taking almost $6 million at American box offices alone.

October, 1963. The third film of the year has Elvis playing two roles – as an Air Force Officer and his hillbilly cousin both at loggerheads over a missile base to be sited in the Smoky Mountains. Made for MGM, *Kissin' Cousins* is produced by Sam Katzman who says, 'I knew that at heart Elvis was a country boy, so I thought we would put him back in the woods where he belonged.' The script has been built around this idea, and the picture proves highly successful, returning its cost of $1.3 million in under a month.

1964

January 12, 1964. Elvis and all the old regulars gather at the RCA Studios in Nashville for a strictly 'studio' session from which come three numbers, 'Memphis, Tennessee', 'Ask Me' and 'It Hurts Me'. The vocals of The Jordanaires are augmented by the splendid Millie Kirkham.

March 6, 1964. Filming begins on *Roustabout* which has Elvis playing a wandering singer who becomes involved in the problems of a troubled carnival show. His co-stars are Barbara Stanwyck and Joan Freeman, but he gets his greatest pleasure from being able to ride a Honda motorbike both on and off the location site of Thousand Oaks in California. Unnoticed among the extras on the picture is a girl destined for international stardom, then making her debut in pictures – Raquel Welch. The album of tunes from *Roustabout*, which Elvis records in Hollywood, becomes another million seller.

July, 1964. With hardly a break, Elvis launches into *Girl Happy* which he films for producer Joe Pasternak in Fort Lauderdale. He plays a night club entertainer who, with his band – Bing Crosby's son Gary, Joby Baker and Jimmy Hawkins – is hired to keep an eye on a rich man's daughter, Shelley Fabares, only to fall in love with her. The eleven songs – including 'Do The Clam' which is released as a single – are all taped in Hollywood.

October 21, 1964. The third film of the year in what is now becoming a regular pattern for Elvis: this is *Tickle Me* for United Artists, directed by old faithful Norman Taurog. Elvis is a rodeo rider who becomes involved in a search for hidden treasure along with two beautiful girls, Julie Adams and Jocelyn Lane. He has nine tunes to sing, including the gutsy 'Dirty, Dirty Feeling', but the picture is disliked by the critics. United Artists, though, make a healthy profit.

1965

February 5, 1965. Three weeks is all it takes to make Elvis' first 'costume' picture, *Harum Scarum*, in which he plays an

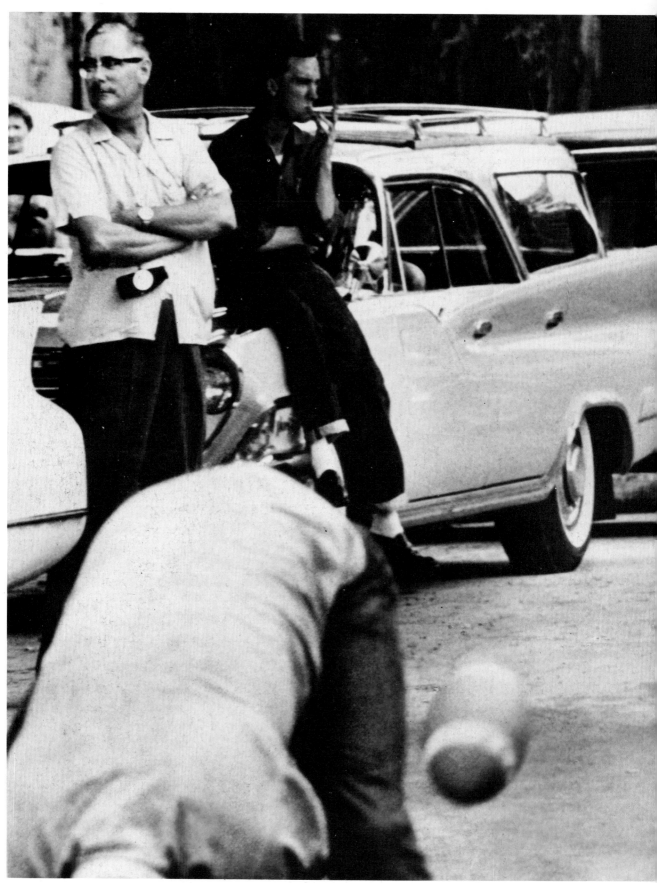

Elvis playing American football in between shots in
Hollywood. He had a team named 'Elvis Presley
Enterprises' which played occasional games.

With the delectable Ursula Andress in *Fun In Acapulco*.

Another beauty who caught Elvis' eye, Ann-Margaret in
Viva Las Vegas.

American movie star kidnapped while touring the Middle East. Although he looks reminiscent of Rudolf Valentino in Arab costume, and earns one million dollars for his work, Elvis sings his eleven tunes well below par. Perhaps the sheer exhaustion of working to Sam Katzman's demanding schedule leaves him unable to raise the necessary enthusiasm when he records in the RCA Studios in Nashville.

April 2, 1965. Elvis and Colonel Tom Parker celebrate their tenth anniversary together, and the manager tells the press that to date his star's pictures have grossed over 125 million dollars, while he has sold in excess of 100 million records for RCA, grossing some 150 million dollars! No mean achievements for a single decade!

May 15, 1965. The famous old story of the riverboat gambler and his temperamental girlfriend, *Frankie and Johnny*, provides Elvis with his next picture – and two delectable co-stars in Nancy Novack and Donna Douglas. This time, however, no one gets killed, although Elvis' performance as the smooth-talking gambler earns him praise from several critics. The famous jazzy title tune is recorded with twelve other songs at United Artists' Studios in Hollywood and released as a single in March 1966.

July 26, 1965. In an attempt to repeat the success of *Blue Hawaii*, Paramount cast Elvis in *Paradise, Hawaiian Style*, in which he plays an airline pilot who goes into business on his own in Hawaii after being sacked for chasing girls. A lot of the location work is shot at the Polynesian Cultural Centre on Oahu, which gives the movie colour and excitement but not quite the same success as its predecessor.

August 27, 1965. 'The King' meets four of his greatest admirers, the fabulously successful Beatles, while they are touring America and also appearing on the Ed Sullivan Show which had been so crucial in Elvis' rise to fame. The five superstars meet at the home Elvis uses while working in Hollywood, on Perugia Way, and, after chatting about their respective careers, play a short jam session in which a highlight is The Beatles' hit 'I Feel Fine', with Elvis playing bass. Says John Lennon afterwards, 'The only person that we wanted to meet in the USA was Elvis Presley. We can't tell you what a thrill that night was for us.' What a thrill it would have been for fans of Elvis or The Beatles if that jam session had been recorded!

1966

February 5, 1966. Elvis chalks up his sixth picture with director Norman Taurog, *Spinout*, for MGM, playing racing driver Mike McCoy, who is subject to the attentions of three beautiful girls, Deborah Walley, Diane McBain and Shelley Fabares. The high-powered cars are matched by some powerful rock 'n' roll singing from Elvis, including the title song and 'Stop, Look And Listen', all recorded at a Hollywood session backed by The Jordanaires. In addition to the nine songs for the picture, Elvis records three more for the album, including his only Bob Dylan song,

'Tomorrow Is A Long Time'.

May 25, 1966. Elvis spends four days in Nashville at the RCA Studios cutting what is to prove a major new religious album, 'How Great Thou Art', with a considerably increased number of musicians, two backing groups and four female vocalists. A new producer also takes over, Felton Jarvis, who is to extend and develop further the superb 'Nashville Sound' that Chet Atkins had given all Elvis' records not tied to the constrictions of a film. These changes have all been introduced to stem the undeniable decline in popularity of Elvis' movie-linked albums. The hard work is rewarded when the album wins a Grammy Award for Best Sacred Performance and also becomes a gold disc just a year after release.

June 10, 1966. Returning to cut three more tracks in Nashville, producer Felton Jarvis has a bright idea to get Elvis in the right mood – despite the heat – to record 'If Every Day Was Like Christmas': he puts a beautifully decorated Christmas tree in the recording studio!

June 19, 1966. As Elvis' next movie, *Double Trouble*, takes place partly in Europe where his character, Guy Lambert, a rock 'n' roll star, is on tour, there is every opportunity for him to film there – but again such ideas are quashed and Norman Taurog films everything on the MGM backlot. Two girls, the provocative Yvonne Romain and the innocent Annette Day, compete for his love, and there is some slapstick comedy from the Wiere Brothers playing three ineffectual foreign policemen. Of the eight songs, only an updated 'Old MacDonald' is in any way memorable.

September 12, 1966. Hal Wallis is again producer on Elvis' third picture of the year, *Easy Come, Easy Go* which gives fans the novel sight of him playing a Navy frogman, Ted Jackson, searching for a sunken treasure ship. The only thing notable about the six-tune EP, recorded in Hollywood and released with the film the following year, is that it is Elvis' last EP as RCA are ceasing production of this type of record.

1967

February 8, 1967. Elvis buys himself a 163-acre ranch in DeSoto County about ten miles south of Graceland, where he can relax and go riding in privacy with Priscilla. He pays $300,000 for the Mississippi property, complete with ranch house and cattle barns – named the 'Circle G Ranch' ('G' for Graceland) – then extensively renovates and enlarges the living and stabling accommodation. The purchase has Elvis dubbed the 'Mississippi Cowboy and Gentleman Rancher', and he spends many happy days on the estate, in particular, riding his favourite horse, Rising Sun.

February 21, 1967. A short trip to Nashville to cut the tunes for *Clambake* before moving to Hollywood to film this United Artists picture which goes before the cameras on

Elvis looking like a new Rudolf Valentino in his first costume picture, *Harum Scarum* made in 1965.

Elvis as rock star, Guy Lambert, with a Beatle-lookalike
backing group in *Double Trouble*.

Elvis 'all at sea' filming *Easy Come, Easy Go* in September 1966.

With one of his most regular and beautiful co-stars,
Shelley Fabares in *Clambake*.

Elvis marries Priscilla Beaulieu in Las Vegas on May 1 1967.

March 6. Playing Scott Heyward, a millionaire's son who changes place with an impoverished ski instructor to win the love of his girl friend, the dependable Shelley Fabares, Elvis acts competently and sings the seven tunes spiritedly.

May 1, 1967. Elvis (now 32) and Priscilla (21) are married in a private suite at the Aladdin Hotel in Las Vegas by Nevada Supreme Court Judge, David Zenoff, a friend of Colonel Parker. Present are Vernon Presley and his wife, Dee, Major and Mrs Beaulieu, a number of close friends and Joe Esposito and Marty Lacker as best men. After a brief press conference and a small reception, the couple honeymoon in Palm Springs. Later, a larger reception for all their friends is held in Memphis on May 28. Elvis also buys a new home for himself and his bride in a sumptuous new estate near Hollywood, so that he will not have far to travel for filming. His new address at 1174 Hillcrest Road, Trousdale, costs him $400,000.

June 15, 1967. The newly-married Elvis returns to work to film *Speedway*, co-starring with his friend Frank Sinatra's daughter, Nancy. He plays a stock car driver with tax troubles who has to win a big race to get out of this fix –and in so doing also wins the heart of Nancy, an undercover investigator on his tail! While making the picture, Elvis announces, 'I'm going to be a father. We hadn't really planned to have a baby this soon, but Priscilla has given me the good news. I was so shocked I didn't think I could move for a while.' And Colonel Parker adds that he has already got a contract drawn up for the new singing Presley! A co-star on the picture, Bill Bixby, comments: 'After he found out he was ecstatic. Elvis was happier than I had seen him.'

September 10, 1967. From a two-day session in Nashville,

Elvis provides some of the best music in years, highlighted by the outstanding guitar playing of Jerry Reed, a protegé of Chet Atkins. Two numbers, 'Big Boss Man' and 'Guitar Man', are considered his best in several years and point towards a new phase in his career.

October 18, 1967. The start of a month's work on *Stay Away, Joe,* a comedy picture for MGM in which Elvis plays a feckless Indian brave who, instead of raising cattle to win a government sponsorship for an entire cattle reservation, is more interested in squandering the money and chasing girls. Elvis is more optimistic about this picture than many of its predecessors. 'It's a more grown-up character,' he says, 'part Hud, part Alfie. In most of my pictures I'm singing in every other scene, but in this one I do only three songs and I get a lot more acting. There isn't a guitar in the whole picture.' For a change, too, the songs are strong and sharp.

November 5, 1967. An auction of unwanted items at the

Circle G Ranch – including a guitar and a blue bath taken from Graceland – raises $100,000 which Elvis donates to charity. His donations to charity are by now legendary.

1968

January 8, 1968. While Elvis is at Graceland with Priscilla, now nearing the end of her pregnancy, Colonel Parker uses the occasion of the singer's birthday to announce that he has just made a deal with NBC Television for a 'Christmas Special' sponsored by Singer Sewing Machines. For this hour-long show, which will mark Elvis' first return to the medium in almost a decade, he is to be paid the astonishing sum of half a million dollars!

February 1, 1968. More good news with the safe birth of a baby girl, weighing 6 lbs 15 ozs, at the Baptist Memorial Hospital in Memphis. Elvis and Priscilla become proud parents at one minute past five in the afternoon and tell the waiting pressmen the girl is to be called Lisa Marie. (If the child had been a boy he would have been called John Baron.) Graceland is deluged with cards and gifts from well-wishers all over the world.

A daughter, Lisa Marie, is born to Priscilla and Elvis on February 1 1968.

An unshaven Elvis on the set of *Charro*.

Another complete change for Elvis – looking very
debonair in *The Trouble With Girls* co-starring Marylyn
Mason.

A moment from the superb NBC TV Special aired on
December 3 1968.

March 11, 1968. Elvis, now a father, returns to Hollywood and work on his next picture, *Live a Little, Love a Little* in which he plays Greg Nolan, a photographer torn between the worlds of glamour and fashion photography. Although few fans spot him when the picture is first released, Vernon Presley appears in a tiny bit part.

June 27, 1968. A milestone day in Elvis' career. After the gradual decline in his sales and popularity through the seemingly endless list of indifferent movies, he goes into the NBC Studios in Burbank to record the Christmas Special which is to become known as his 'Comeback'. Producer Steve Binder is in no doubt about the importance of this show. 'I felt very, very strongly that this was Elvis' moment of truth,' he says later. 'If he did another movie-type thing he would wipe out his career and be known only as a fifties phenomenon. On the other hand, if he could do a special and prove he was still number one, he could have a whole rejuvenation thing going.' A superb selection of songs ranging across Elvis' career, plus a fantastic black leather outfit for the show, make this Special a real turning point in his life. It is not achieved without nerves and sweat, however, as Elvis admits. 'I haven't been in front of a live audience in eight years,' he says. 'What am I going to do if they don't like me?'

July 22, 1968. Another complete change for Elvis in his next picture, *Charro*, which he makes for National General Pictures, playing an unshaven and ruthless outlaw on the trail of his former gang who have stolen a priceless gold and silver cannon. Despite his appearance and the fact that he does not sing a single tune in the picture, Elvis tells the press, 'I don't think I'm changing my image, I just think you have to mature a little bit.'

October 15, 1968. From the scruffiness of *Charro* to the style of *The Trouble with Girls*, the MGM picture in which Elvis plays Walter Hale, the manager of a dancing troupe who sports a dashing white suit and hat. There is a debonair touch to his acting, too, and a stronger hint of sexuality (with Marylyn Mason) than in any of his previous movies. Marylyn duets with Elvis on 'Sign of the Zodiac', while he gives a fine solo recording of 'Swing Low, Sweet Chariot'.

December 3, 1968. On a Tuesday evening at 9 pm the much-heralded TV Special is broadcast, and Elvis' performance is heaped with praise. The *New York Times* calls his show 'charismatic' and Jon Landau of *Eye* magazine sums up the feelings of millions of viewers when he writes, 'There is something magical about watching a man who has lost himself find his way back home. He sang with the kind of power people no longer expect from rock 'n' roll singers.' And *Record World* adds, 'It was a modish performance, virile and humorous and vibrating with the nervousness of the times.' To top off the praise, Elvis learns that in Britain, the readers of the leading pop newspaper, *New Musical Express*, have voted him 'Best Vocalist of the Year'. What a year 1968 has proved to be! Elvis himself later comments, 'I'm now planning a lot of changes. You can't go on doing the same thing year after year. I don't want to do so many pictures and I'm thinking about making some personal appearance tours.'

1969

January 13, 1969. The start of what are to prove two major recording sessions for Elvis in his home town of Memphis in the American Recording Studio – the first such, in fact, since he recorded for Sam Phillips at Sun. These sessions have been switched at the last moment from Nashville, and bring in a whole new group of personnel as musicians and vocalists. The highlights of this first session (the second runs from February 17 to 22) are 'Long Black Limousine', 'I'll Hold You In My Heart', 'Stranger In My Home Town', 'After Loving You' and the masterpiece 'Suspicious Minds'. These sessions gave Elvis the unique achievement of two gold albums and three multi-million singles: his greatest ever triumph. To his fans he is walking on water again: in practice he and Priscilla have slipped away for a month's vacation to Aspen, Colorado, where Elvis learns to ski!

March 5, 1969. As Elvis begins work on his Universal International picture, *Change of Habit*, his new single, the evocative protest song, 'In The Ghetto', soars into the charts, eventually reaching number three and selling 1,500,000 copies – his best for years. By a strange quirk of fate, Elvis is playing a doctor, John Carpenter, working in the slums, in *Change of Habit*. Co-starring with him is Mary Tyler Moore as a nurse who is actually a nun without her habit. While in Hollywood Elvis records five tunes for the movie, and for the first time in years is available for interviews to certain US and British journalists.

July 5, 1969. Following the stunning success of his TV Special, the now re-heralded 'King of Rock 'n' Roll' travels to Las Vegas to begin rehearsals for his first public appearance in a decade at the newly opened International Hotel.

July 31, 1969. First night for Elvis in the International Hotel's 2,000 capacity 'Showroom Internationale' – following Barbra Streisand who had opened the hotel the previous two weeks. Elvis receives $1 million for his four-week engagement and delights the packed first night audience with the joke that he is here because he 'got tired of singing to the guys I beat up in my motion pictures.' His magnificent performance leaves the audience cheering for more as he attends a press conference and tells the assembled newsmen, 'I missed the live contact with an audience. Now I want to play all over the world.' The music critics are unanimous in their praise, *Newsweek* summarising the feelings of them all: 'The most incredible thing about Elvis is his staying power in a world where meteoric careers fade like shooting stars.' By the end of the engagement, Elvis has been seen by 101,500 customers! RCA have also taped several of the shows, and issue Elvis' first live album 'In Person' as well as his first double LP 'From Memphis to Vegas'.

Elvis signing autographs while filming *Change of Habit*.

November 4, 1969. 'Suspicious Minds', released as a single, reaches the number one spot in the American charts –Elvis' first top disc in seven years. This is followed by 'Don't Cry, Daddy' (which Elvis recorded because it reminded him of his mother) which reaches number six, also selling well over a million copies.

1970

January 26, 1970. Elvis opens his second season at the International Hotel in a new outfit fit for a king – a white jump suit with a high collar covered in semi-precious jewels. Booked almost solid before the engagement begins, the hotel can boast: 'Elvis Presley is the greatest box office attraction the world has ever known. That goes for this generation or any generation. Caruso and Valentino never drew like Elvis.' Indeed he has drawn fans from as far away as Britain, Europe, Australia and Japan, some of whom attend every one of the 29 days of double shows. He includes a number of songs made popular by other artists in his repertoire, and again several shows are taped by RCA between February 16 to 19 for a second live album.

February 28, 1970. More show business records tumble when Elvis flies to Houston to play six concerts in the incredible 44,500 seater Astrodrome, nicknamed 'The eighth wonder of the world'. Earning something in excess of $1.2 million for his shows – even with tickets scaled down to $1 so that even the poorer fans can get in – Elvis is assuredly top of the tree, as Colonel Tom Parker is quick to tell the press. 'To maintain his image as "The King", Presley needs "super engagements",' he says. 'By appearing in Las Vegas' biggest showroom and in the Astrodrome, he has just that.' Elvis himself has also wanted to go back to East Texas because it was there that fans really started to boost his career back in 1954 and 1955.

June 4, 1970. Elvis spends four days in his old haunt, the RCA Studios in Nashville – but with a new generation of local musicians – to cut 34 new tunes from which will come a pair of two million-selling albums and a top ten hit.

July 6, 1970. With posters going up all over Las Vegas and in the International Hotel announcing Elvis' third season – 'Elvis Summer Festival', it is called – filming also starts of *Elvis: That's The Way It Is*, MGM's movie of Elvis from rehearsal to final performance. The picture is directed by the talented Denis Sanders, who explains his purpose. 'What we're trying to do is capture Elvis the entertainer from the point of view of the fans, the hotel and the audience. About half the film will be edited from Elvis's first five performances at the Showroom and the rest will be scenes of fans and interviews. What I'm shooting is a musical documentary.'

Elvis at a press conference in August 1969 announcing his return to live appearances at the Las Vegas International.

1971

August 10, 1970. Another sell-out season for Elvis at the International, with the MGM film cameras capturing the best moments. RCA, too, issue an album based on the performances, and once again there is an unofficial 'bootleg' LP called 'King of Las Vegas Live' which enjoys widespread success. At the conclusion of the Hotel dates, Elvis goes back on the road again on September 9, for the first time in over 13 years. He does six performances in six days at Phoenix, Detroit, St Louis, Miami, Tampa and Mobile. In November he plays another eight dates from Oakland to Denver where he finishes on the 17th.

December 21, 1970. On a sudden impulse, Elvis goes to Washington to deliver personally a letter he has written expressing his beliefs about Communism and drugs to President Nixon, half hoping he may have an interview with the President. To his delight, this is granted and he spends some time talking to the President. The two men are photographed shaking hands, and Nixon makes Elvis a federal narcotics agent in appreciation of his views about drugs.

January 16, 1971. The triumphs of the previous year continue when Elvis is named one of seven 'Outstanding Young Men of the Year' by the American Junior Chambers of Commerce. The presentations this year take place, appropriately, in the Memphis Municipal Auditorium, which Elvis had visited as a child to hear concerts. His family and friends are present for the ceremony. In accepting his award, Elvis says, 'I'd like you folks to know that when I was young I was the hero of the comic book. I saw movies and I was the hero of the movie. So every dream that I ever dreamed has come true a hundred times.' And in thanking the group for his nomination, he ends by breaking into song: 'I learned very early in life – "Without a song, the day would never end; without a song, a man ain't got no friend; without a song, the world would've never been; without a song" – so I'll keep singing a song. Goodnight.' One of Elvis' very rare attendances at an official ceremony also proves one of his most moving.

January 26, 1971. The opening of another season at the International Hotel – this one overshadowed by a death threat to Elvis. A telephone caller says a gunman is planning to kill him during a performance and offers to reveal the assassin's name for $50,000. The FBI provide protection

1. A young man destined for immortality – an early shot
of Elvis recording.

2. Elvis' rippin' it up – another early photograph from 1957.

3. Moody and magnificent: an early pin-up photo of Elvis.

5. Elvis with co-star Dolores Hart in *Loving You* in 1957.

4. About to hit the screen big-time: Elvis in Hollywood.

6. The inviting East – in a Hollywood studio! Elvis in *Harum Scarum* (1965).

Sincerely
Season's Greetings
Elvis
and
Colonel

7. Elvis and Colonel Parker pose for one of their light-hearted Christmas cards!

14. Keepin' in shape! Elvis practising Karate to enable him to perform some of his strenuous stage routines.

16. Not an ending – for the music goes on . . .

15. 'The King' looking the part!

12. (*Above*) Elvis with Priscilla and their daughter Lisa Marie.

13. Vernon Presley and his son share a moment during a concert in 1977.

9/10. Shots from two of Elvis' great television specials. (*Above*) The NBC show 'Elvis' shown in December 1968; and (*left*) delighting his world-wide audience in the satellite TV show 'Aloha From Hawaii' in January 1973.

11. Elvis doing what he does best – making records.

8. Elvis in the Army – catching up on the news from back
home while in Germany.

Elvis being filmed for the movie, *That's The Way It Is* in
July 1970.

Elvis 'the greatest box office attraction the world has ever known' in the International Hotel in 1970.

and those close to Elvis watch him with great care. Thankfully, nothing materialises.

May 15, 1971. After an aborted session two months earlier (cancelled because Elvis had an eye infection), the RCA Studios are alive to the sound of thirty tracks which the singer makes for a new Christmas album – although his superb rendering of Bob Dylan's classic, 'Don't Think Twice', hardly fits in such company. Because he is unhappy with one or two of the tracks, Elvis returns to Nashville on June 8 to record eight more religious songs which will be used for an LP, 'He Touched Me', to accompany 'The Wonderful World of Christmas'.

July 20, 1971. Elvis breaks new ground playing the Sahara Tahoe Club on Lake Tahoe, Nevada, breaking showroom records by attracting 3,400 people for the dinner and midnight shows on July 27. Back home he learns that Highway 51, which runs directly in front of Graceland, has been renamed Elvis Presley Boulevard to mark his achievements.

August 9, 1971. It is another month of sold-out shows at the International Hotel for Elvis, where this particular stint is highlighted by another prestigious honour, the Bing Crosby Award, given by the National Academy of Recording Arts and Sciences for his 'outstanding creative and artistic contributions of long-lasting duration in the field of phonograph recordings.' In getting this highest honour in music, he joins other 'greats' such as Duke Ellington, Ella Fitzgerald, Irving Berlin and his friend, Frank Sinatra. Coincidental with this, columnist May Mann suggests that, because of his enormous following and charisma, Elvis should run for President, writing in a widely syndicated piece: 'Elvis has honesty, sincerity, integrity, a well-known fine character, a love for his country and fellow man; he has guts, courage, and assurance; and he is a born leader! Who else?' The idea might well have appealed to Elvis, but it develops no further.

October 24, 1971. A 12-hour-radio special, 'The Elvis Presley Story', by Jerry Hopkins, featuring interviews with people who knew the singer during various periods of his life, is broadcast complete in New York. In other parts of the country and abroad it is broken into segments, usually of two hours each. According to producer Ron Jacobs, when Elvis learns of this special he comments, 'What do they want to do 12 hours on *me* for?'

November 5, 1971. The year closes with fourteen shows in twelve days in the East and Midwest from Minneapolis to Salt Lake City. The sell-out performances net in excess of $1,500,000!

Elvis reunited with his boyhood heroes, J. D. Sumner and The Stamps for his 1972 season in Las Vegas.

Informal moment from The King's final movie, *Elvis On Tour* shot in 1972.

1972

January 26, 1972. For his new season at the International Hotel, Elvis recruits the famous gospel group, J. D. Sumner and The Stamps Quartet, whom he has admired since his youth. RCA record the shows from February 14 to 17, but the song selected for single release, 'An American Trilogy', proves a flop. The show, however, is praised by Frank Lieberman of the *Los Angeles Herald-Examiner* who calls Elvis a 'devastating showman; confident, compelling and always in control'.

February 23, 1972. Although Elvis and Priscilla have been drifting apart, he is shattered when she decides to leave him. As his close friend, Ed Parker, says later, 'The biggest setback in Elvis' life was the death of his mother, but the biggest threat to his ego was the loss of his wife. Had Priscilla died, he could have coped, but to lose her to another man was a mortal blow.' Elvis again professes his love for his wife, but senses he has lost her to Karate instructor Mike Stone.

March 27, 1972. While starting work on what is to prove his final film, *Elvis On Tour*, MGM's perceptive and revealing look at the singer at work and play, in concert as

well as recording, Elvis cuts a poignant track, 'Separate Ways', in the RCA Studios in Hollywood. This song, about his parting from Priscilla, has been written by his friend, Red West, and he sings with obvious emotion. The documentary film is produced by Pierre Adidge and directed by Robert Abel who both feel they are 'recording a phenomenon for posterity'. Their clever use of earlier television material, still photographs, snatches of interviews and cuts from performances on the April 5 to 19 tour, results in a motion picture which lives up totally to Colonel Parker's instructions to 'make the best Elvis Presley movie anybody ever made'. And that, quite simply, is what *Elvis On Tour* remains to this day – a tribute and a memorial to 'The King of Rock 'n' Roll'. (Deservedly, too, this film wins a Golden Globe Award in 1973.)

June 9, 1972. Elvis climbs one of the last great show business mountains – playing for the first time the far-famed Madison Square Garden in New York. Of the opening of his four shows at this venue, *Variety* represents the view of the assembled critics when it states, 'Presley is now a highly polished, perfectly timed, spectacularly successful show business machine.' Such is the outstanding success of this concert that RCA rush out an LP of the show in its entirety just three days later, and over a million copies are sold. With Elvis drawing $730,000 at the box office for the four shows, plus his usual percentage on the record sales, it is estimated he has made $1.2 million for six hours' singing!

Nothing else on the remainder of the tour, which winds up in Tulsa on June 20, can quite match this incredible achievement.

August 18, 1972. During what will be his final season at the International Hotel in Las Vegas, Elvis files a lawsuit in the Santa Monica Divorce Court. The break-up of his marriage to Priscilla is said to have been caused by 'irreconcilable differences' and it is agreed that she will have custody of four-year-old Lisa. Three months later, in November, Elvis winds up the year with an eight-stop tour closing in Honolulu on November 18.

1973

January 14, 1973. Another splendid and quite amazing moment in Elvis' life when a satellite TV show from Hawaii is seen by an estimated audience of 500 million viewers all over the world. A year in the planning, this hour-long show, 'Aloha From Hawaii', is beamed via satellite at 1 am from the International Centre Arena in Honolulu, to allow it to be seen live in Australia, Japan and much of the Far East. The following night it is seen by 28 European countries. RCA again rush out a double album of the complete concert, selling two million copies. Cost of the spectacle is later estimated at $2.5 million – the most expensive entertainment special ever done – Elvis making $1 million for his two hours' work. The two shows he puts on in Hawaii also raise in excess of $85,000 for the Kui Lee Cancer Fund.

April 4, 1973. NBC screen a ninety-minute version of 'Aloha From Hawaii' which gets 57 per cent of the viewing audience and is described as a 'stunning and rare moment in television' by the *Los Angeles Times*. NBC also announce plans for three more specials, the first in Japan, a second in London and – most ambitious of all – a third in Moscow. Sadly, these are never to materialise . . .

July 21, 1973. Amidst his busy schedule of tours and hotel showroom appearances, Elvis goes back to Memphis to spend four days in a recording studio: his first such visit in almost two years. He uses the Stax Studio, famous for its rhythm and blues successes, and there is a strong flavour of this about several of the songs he records. There is also, though, a general sense of depression about the recordings and Elvis himself is evidently very down, his health declining through an increasing dependence on medication and over-eating.

August 6, 1973. A month of dates for Elvis at the Las Vegas Hilton where over 100,000 people pay to see his twice-daily shows. His overweight condition is, however, drawing comment from the critics who also sense a disinterest from him about his performances. He does not disappoint his fans, nonetheless . . .

October 15, 1973. Elvis enters the Baptist Memorial Hospital in Memphis for rest and treatment to a recurring pneumonia

that makes breathing difficult. When word of this gets out, the hospital is deluged with get-well cards and flowers from all over the world. He finally leaves the hospital on November 1, and rounds off the year with another recording session from December 10 to 16 at Stax when he cuts 18 songs with something like his old enthusiasm – although there is an undoubted sadness about many of his choices.

1974

January 8, 1974. Celebrating his 39th birthday, Elvis learns that the Governor of Georgia, Jimmy Carter, has declared this to be 'Elvis Presley Day' in the state. Carter, of course, is later to become President of the USA. RCA also mark the event by releasing the first volume of an LP, 'Elvis – A Legendary Performer', with songs and musical milestones from his career, which proves an instant hit and leads to two follow-up volumes. (This success is also to lead the company to package other of its top stars in the same way.)

March 6, 1974. After another stint at the Las Vegas Hilton, Elvis goes on a 25-performance tour of fourteen cities in the South, and while in Alabama, Governor George Wallis goes one better than his opposite number in Georgia by declaring the next seven days 'Elvis Presley Week'. Arriving in Memphis on March 20, RCA take the opportunity to record his performance at the Midsouth Coliseum for a new album, 'Elvis Recorded Live on Stage in Memphis' – but this proves disappointing because of the proliferation of so many of his old songs.

April 4, 1974. An Australian promoter offers $1,000,000 to Colonel Parker for Elvis to play just *two* concerts in that country. The Colonel responds, 'Thank you, but if we ever need a million bucks that badly we'll give you a ring.' He also turns down a similar offer for just a single concert from a London impresario offering Wembley Stadium as a venue.

July, 1974. Elvis draws up plans to make a movie comeback about his great passion, Karate. Early ideas are for a documentary about the sport narrated by Elvis, but this is changed to an adventure story with Elvis starring as a retired CIA agent running a Karate school seeking revenge for the murder of a friend by drug dealers. Although a script is written by Rick Husky, the project founders.

1975

January 8, 1975. Another milestone in Elvis' life – his 40th birthday – and fans organise a bumper celebration to mark forty years of his life, twenty-one of them as 'The King'. Despite attacks in several newspapers and magazines about his increasing waistline and decreasing skill as a performer and recording artist, Elvis receives good wishes by the thousand from his loyal admirers.

March 9, 1975. After almost six months of seclusion – giving rise, perhaps inevitably, to newspaper stories that he is now

America's most famous recluse after Howard Hughes – Elvis spends three days in the RCA Studios in Hollywood producing ten tracks, including the fine rock numbers, 'T-r-o-u-b-l-e' and 'I Can Help'. After these sessions he flies to Las Vegas for a fortnight in concert at the Hilton, these dates coinciding with the release of a new album of classic songs called 'Pure Gold' which appropriately soon sells one million copies.

May 3, 1975. A heavy schedule of concerts takes Elvis for two weeks to some of his earliest stamping grounds in the South, and his generosity is demonstrated yet again when he plays a benefit for victims of a tornado in Mississippi, which raises $110,000.

July 27, 1975. An extraordinary day in the Presley legend when he buys no less than fourteen cars from the Madison Cadillac Agency in Memphis! His interest in cars has always been intense, and over the years of his fame Elvis has owned several hundred expensive cars of one sort or another, at a cost of over one million dollars! Not long after this, he buys a Convair 880 Jet for $1 million and spends almost this much again remodelling the plane as a 'flying palace.' The jet carries his personal symbol, a bolt of lightning and the initials TCB (Taking Care of Business), and is named after his daughter, Lisa Marie.

December 2, 1975. After a break of over three months, Elvis reappears at the Las Vegas Hilton playing to packed audiences for every show. During his absence it transpires he has been offered the lead role opposite Barbra Streisand in *A Star Is Born*, a projected remake of the Judy Garland classic. For various reasons this falls through – just as had earlier a scheme to star him in a stage version of the life of Rudolf Valentino, for which he was reputedly offered $2,500,000! Unhappily, his now acute weight problem would certainly have prevented this coming to fruition.

December 31, 1975. Despite the problems of the previous year, Elvis sees in 1976 playing for the very first – and last – time during his winter holidays at a special concert in the 80,000-seater Silver Dome in Pontiac, Michigan. Although the biting cold makes it difficult for Elvis and his musicians to give of their best – and he even splits his pants at one stage – he has the satisfaction of setting a record which remains unsurpassed to this day. The event takes $816,000 for the performance – the highest amount for a single night by a single artist, topping even the record of The Beatles at Shea Stadium in 1964.

1976

February 2, 1976. After holidaying at the ski resort of Vail in Colorado – where he delights in driving snowmobiles – Elvis finds a new location for recording: his den in Graceland! Equipment is installed in the house by RCA and, with his usual Nashville musicians and producer Fleton Jarvis, Elvis cuts 12 tracks which are released in May as an album, 'From Elvis Presley Boulevard'. The songs are almost without exception sad and all too clearly show Elvis' failing health.

April 21, 1976. As his part in the American Bicentennial celebrations, Elvis makes a crosscountry tour beginning in Kansas City and taking in Long Beach on the West Coast before moving through New England in late July and through Chicago and the Mid-West in October. The *Los Angeles Times* calls the tour 'a combination of music and manner that often resembles more a visit among friends than a hard-edged concert performance.'

August 21, 1976. RCA issue a press release with the staggering statistic that Elvis' record sales have just passed the 400 million mark, a feat unequalled by any other artist living or dead.

August 23, 1976. Elvis' autumn season at the Las Vegas Hilton is cancelled after three nights due to his ill-health. But he returns to the hotel on December 1 and plays 12 days of powerful shows, although his appearance worries friends and fans alike.

October 29, 1976. RCA set up recording facilities once more in Graceland and Elvis cuts five tunes, one of these, 'Pledging My Love' – being appropriate vis-a-vis his developing romance with 20-year-old beauty queen Ginger Alden. Another, 'He'll Have To Go', is quite the opposite as it is to be among his last recordings.

1977

January 26, 1977. Elvis becomes engaged to Ginger Alden at Graceland, presenting her with an eleven-and-a-half carat gold ring valued at $70,000.

February 12, 1977. After an abortive attempt to record some more songs, first at Nashville in January and then in the mobile unit installed once again by RCA in Graceland in the first week of February, Elvis begins his shortest scheduled tour – nine shows in nine days in southern cities he has not visited previously: Miami, West Palm Beach, Orlando, Augusta and Columbia in South Carolina. His overweight makes the performances listless and well below his usual standard.

March 4, 1977. Elvis flies in the *Lisa Marie* to Hawaii for a 14-day vacation, staying in a beach house in Kailua. The rest seems to improve his health and he returns to America for a tour that is to take him back through the parts of

Texas, Arkansas and Louisiana where he learned his art and gained his first fans.

March 31, 1977. Despite a determined effort to capture some of his old magic in his 'heartland', Elvis falls ill again and fails to appear at a concert in Louisiana State University in Baton Rouge. Instead he flies back to Memphis and a spell in the Baptist Hospital.

April 20, 1977. Another tour, starting from Columbia and finishing in St Paul ten days later, attracts huge crowds as always – but also some of the harshest criticisms so far from reviewers who call him 'old, fat and with a voice that cracks'. At best, says one critic, he is now just a parody of his former self. Though his performances certainly lack the fire of his earlier work, it is becoming evident that the press feel the best stories about Elvis these days are the cruellest ones.

April 25, 1977. While appearing at the Civic Centre in Saginaw, RCA tape three of Elvis' numbers, 'If You Love Me', a humorous version of 'Little Darlin' and a whole-hearted rendering of 'Unchained Melody' in which the only accompaniment is by Elvis himself on piano.

May 29, 1977. Looking tired, his voice weak, Elvis walks off stage in mid-performance in front of 13,000 people in the Baltimore Civic Centre. However, after a thirty minute break he reappears to rapturous applause and completes his show with five more songs. It is, nevertheless, an ominous occurrence . . .

June 2, 1977. After two more concerts in Macon, Georgia and Mobile, Alabama, Elvis returns to Memphis to rest once more. Colonel Parker announces that after a 12-day tour beginning in Portland on August 17 and culminating – as so often before – in Memphis on August 28, Elvis will have at least two clear months doing nothing. In the interim, he is to make another TV Special scheduled for an October 3 showing.

June 19, 1977. CBS Television start the first of two days' filming of Elvis on tour for their Special, *Elvis In Concert.* Preliminary filming is done in Omaha, with the second part in Rapid City on June 21. Producers Bill Harbach and Gary Smith catch some of his best moments on stage, and inter-cut these with interviews with fans along with all the paraphernalia that goes with an Elvis Presley live show. Elvis cannot disguise his overweight – indeed he jokes about it with the audience in Rapid City – but appears to be in good spirits.

June 25, 1977. In the Market Square Arena in Cincinnati Elvis plays what is to be his last concert. Those present at this sad event – though no one knows it is to be such at the time – testify to the energy and driving strength Elvis puts into his act and his singing. His repertoire ranges across the many hits of his career, and apart from introducing the members of his band and vocalists, he also acknowledges

his father and Ginger Alden who are in the auditorium. He closes with 'Can't Help Falling In Love' and even the press have to concede that the show was 'dynamite'.

August 1, 1977. Publication of *Elvis: What Happened?,* the paperback book by two of Elvis' disgruntled former employees, Red and Sonny West, which deeply upsets him with its allegations of drug abuse and wild eccentricity. Serialisation of the story in a mass-circulation American newspaper further splashes the sensationalised biography, which similarly enrages millions of fans.

August 3, 1977. Elvis is lifted from his gloom by the arrival of his nine-year-old daughter, Lisa Marie, for whom he hires a local theme park, Libertyland, on August 7, so that they can enjoy the rides in privacy. They also go on a shopping spree in Memphis. It is to be the last time anyone sees him alive in the city he has made world famous.

August 15, 1977. Elvis spends the day with Lisa Marie at Graceland, and also discusses his next scheduled tour – already a sell-out and due to begin in two days at Portland, Maine – with one of his associates, Dick Grob. Obviously still upset by all the furore caused by *Elvis: What Happened?,* he tells Grob, 'Dick we'll just show them how wrong they are. We'll make this tour the best ever.' They are to prove his last poignant words.

August 16, 1977. Just before 2 pm, Ginger Alden discovers Elvis slumped on the floor of his bathroom in Graceland. By his side lies a book he was reading, *The Face of Jesus* by Frank Adams. There is no sign of life, and although a doctor and ambulance are summoned and rush Elvis to the Baptist Memorial Hospital, he never recovers consciousness. Vernon Presley is first informed of the death of his son and then, at 3.30 pm, the announcement is made to the world that Elvis Presley, aged 42, the undisputed 'King of Rock 'n' Roll', has passed into immortality. The subsequent coverage of this tragedy by all the media is truly enormous, matched only in recent times by the assassination of President Kennedy.

August 18, 1977. Crowds estimated at over 100,000, many of them still numb with shock like other fans around the world, crowd into Memphis for Elvis' funeral service at Graceland. Only members of the Presley family and close friends – a total of just under 200 – are present at the actual ceremony at 2 pm in the Music Room. Pastor C.W. Bradley of the Whitehaven Church of Christ delivers the eulogy. He says, 'Elvis can serve as an inspiring example of the great potential of one human being who has strong desire and unfailing determination. From total obscurity he rose to world fame. His name is a household word in every nook and corner of this Earth. Though idolised by millions and forced to be protected from crowds, Elvis never lost his desire to stay in close touch with humanity.' And he adds, 'But Elvis was a frail human being. And he would be the first to admit his weaknesses. Perhaps because of his rapid rise to fame and fortune he was thrown into temptation

Making a joke at his own expense just six weeks before his death, Elvis in military hat and his 'Pizza Suit'.

Memphis Press-Scimitar

U.S. WEATHER FORECAST: A 60 per cent chance of rain with high in the upper 80s. Low tonight low 70s. High Thursday mid 80s.

97TH YEAR   MEMPHIS, TENN., WEDNESDAY, AUGUST 17, 1977   TELEPHONES: NEWS AND GENERAL 526-2141   CIRCULATION 525-7801   WANT ADS 526-8892

SPECIAL EDITION

Memphis Leads the World in Mourning the Monarch of Rock 'n Roll

A Lonely Life Ends on Elvis Presley Boulevard

By CLARK PORTEOUS
Press-Scimitar Staff Writer

(Aug. 17, 1977)

The King is dead.

Elvis Presley — the jiggling, jiving, rock 'n roll king — lived just 42 years, seven months and eight days.

It was an exciting but frustrating life which ended in Baptist Hospital, where Elvis was pronounced dead at 3:30 p.m. yesterday of a heart attack.

Elvis made millions of dollars and literally was worshiped by millions of fans. But he was lonesome much of the time, paid a high price for privacy and could not do many things he would have liked to do because he always drew a crowd of admirers.

Elvis, with a pleasant singing voice and a new style, strumming a guitar and gyrating his pelvis — which brought him the name in early days of "Elvis the Pelvis" — made millions, was able to buy anything he wanted, yet happiness seemed to elude him.

Elvis gave away countless thousands, giving funds to numerous Memphis institutions just before Christmas every year. He would give his friends — and occasionally even strangers — expensive automobiles.

Yet as the years passed, many of his friends seemed to have faded away, not generally because they wanted to, but some said Elvis had changed.

Elvis Aron Presley was written about on his 40th birthday, and friends were quoted as saying he was "fat and forty" and refused to see anybody until his weight got down to his regular trim 180 pounds. He was staying in his mansion, Graceland, on Elvis Presley Boulevard, a part of Bellevue renamed by city fathers to honor Elvis.

He became more and more of a recluse in his last few years. Red West and other close friends, who used to be called the "Memphis Mafia," were no longer with him.

Elvis, already a living legend and somewhat of a folk hero to many, was found unconscious at Graceland at 2:30 p.m. yesterday.

Maurice Elliott, Baptist Hospital vice president, said Joe Esposito, Presley's road manager and long-time friend, called an ambulance and tried to revive Elvis with mouth-to-mouth resuscitation and heart massage until the ambulance ar-

A Tribute to Elvis

The unexpected death of rock 'n roll star Elvis Presley Aug. 16, 1977, was news of international impact. Almost every news agency in the world reported the tragedy under a Memphis dateline.

The public interest required that many members of *The Press-Scimitar* staff have a hand in compiling and presenting the story. Every conceivable angle was covered in a period of five publication days. Requests for copies of *The Press-Scimitar* containing coverage of the singer's death poured in from all over the world in great numbers. It was impossible to meet the demand.

Therefore, as a public service to its readers, *The Press-Scimitar* has reprinted in this special tribute edition all Elvis Presley stories and pictures published in the five-day period. With as few changes as possible, all stories and pictures that we published in the regular editions of *The Press-Scimitar* are reprinted herein. This edition plus a similar edition of *The Commercial Appeal* are offered to readers for 50 cents.

"Goodbye, darling, goodbye — I loved you so much," a sobbing Elvis said before leaving the burial site. "I lived my whole life just for you."

Elvis once recalled that in his boyhood his mother was very possessive of him, probably due to the loss of the twin. The Presleys had no other children.

"My mama never let me out of her sight," Elvis said. "I couldn't go down to the creek with the other kids. Sometimes, when I was little, I used to run off. Mama would whip me and I thought she didn't love me."

Elvis knew extreme poverty as well as extreme wealth.

His father, Vernon, who has shared in his son's success, did odd jobs and farmed in Tupelo, but the family was poor. When Elvis was 14, the family moved to Memphis. They lived in a one-room apartment on Alabama in North Memphis at first, later moved into Lauderdale Courts, one of the two first public housing projects built in Memphis in the mid-'30s.

Elvis was graduated from Humes in 1953. He had been too small to make the football team, but he was interested in sports and learned to be an expert at karate.

After graduation from Humes, Elvis worked on the assembly line of a precision tool company, then at a furniture factory making plastic tables and then as a truck driver for Crown Electric Co. He also ushered at Loew's State, a theater which was later to show many of his movies.

In the summer of 1953, Elvis took the step which led to fame and fortune. He had "just an urgin'" and went to Sam Phillips' Sun Record Co. He paid to have a recording made for his mother. Elvis said "it sounded like somebody beating on a bucket lid." But Elvis was told he had an unusual voice and someone might call him.

Months passed and Elvis kept driving a truck for $35 a week. At night he attended a trade school, studying to be an electrician.

Then in the spring of 1954, lightning

ELVIS PRESLEY: THE BEAT WENT ON — AND ON AND ON

— UPI Telephoto

Mourners In Waiting For Last Homecoming Of Revered Singer

By CHARLES GOODMAN and HENRY BAILEY
Press-Scimitar Staff Writers

the crowd, which had surged forward. A hearse entered behind police motorcycles, and the crowd watched as a copper casket was carried up the steps of Graceland and

MOURNER AT GRACELAND

— Staff Photo by William L. Leaptrott

---

that some never experience. Elvis would not want anyone to think that he had no flaws or faults. But now he's gone, I find it more helpful to remember his good qualities, and I hope you do, too.' The body of Elvis is then taken the short distance to Forest Hill Cemetery and laid to rest beside that of his mother.

October 2, 1977. Because of the enormous number of fans visiting Elvis' grave in Forest Hill Cemetery – estimates put the figure at over one million in the first month after his death – and because of the arrest of three men suspected of trying to steal Elvis' body and hold it for ransom – the coffins containing both the singer and his mother are removed and reburied in what is designated the Meditation Gardens at Graceland. Here 'The King' lies to this day . . .

December 6, 1977. The first of many memorials to Elvis takes place when Highway 78, the arterial road running between Tupelo and Memphis – the road which symbolically carried Elvis from poverty to riches and fame almost beyond belief – is renamed 'The Elvis Aaron Presley Memorial Highway' and formally opened at a special

ceremony. Another measure of Elvis' achievement is underlined when RCA Records issue some statistics about his record sales during the 22 years he was with the label. At this time he has sold more than 600,000,000 singles and albums internationally; had 55 million-selling singles, with

The tombstone reads:

✝

ELVIS AARON PRESLEY

JANUARY 8, 1935
AUGUST 16, 1977

SON OF
VERNON ELVIS PRESLEY
AND
GLADYS LOVE PRESLEY
FATHER OF
LISA MARIE PRESLEY

HE WAS A PRECIOUS GIFT FROM GOD
WE CHERISHED AND LOVED DEARLY.

HE HAD A GOD-GIVEN TALENT THAT HE SHARED
WITH THE WORLD. AND WITHOUT A DOUBT,
HE BECAME MOST WIDELY ACCLAIMED;
CAPTURING THE HEARTS OF YOUNG AND OLD ALIKE.

HE WAS ADMIRED NOT ONLY AS AN ENTERTAINER,
BUT AS THE GREAT HUMANITARIAN THAT HE WAS;
FOR HIS GENEROSITY, AND HIS KIND FEELINGS
FOR HIS FELLOW MAN.

HE REVOLUTIONIZED THE FIELD OF MUSIC AND
RECEIVED ITS HIGHEST AWARDS.

HE BECAME A LIVING LEGEND IN HIS OWN TIME,
EARNING THE RESPECT AND LOVE OF MILLIONS.

GOD SAW THAT HE NEEDED SOME REST AND
CALLED HIM HOME TO BE WITH HIM.

WE MISS YOU, SON AND DADDY. I THANK GOD
THAT HE GAVE US YOU AS OUR SON.

VERNON PRESLEY

Elvis is laid to rest in Graceland in a magnificent tomb.

'Hound Dog' and 'Don't Be Cruel' topping this list at over 8,000,000 each. Of his albums, 24 have been certified gold records, 'Blue Hawaii' the chart leader with over 5,000,000. His 33 films have grossed more than $150,000,000, and since he resumed personal appearances in 1969, he has averaged 50 one-night shows at an average gross of $100,000. RCA believe that the total gross of Elvis Presley's entertainment activities is 'in excess of $4.3 billion'!

1978

February 21, 1978. Surprisingly, a Broadway show based on Elvis' life, *The Legend Lives,* lasts for only two months, despite a fine impersonation of 'The King' by Rick Saucedo and the appearance of some musicians who played with him – the vocal group, The Jordanaires, and his accompanist, Kathy Westmoreland. This is in stark contrast to London, where a stage musical, *Elvis,* attracts packed houses and wins the *Evening Standard* 'Best Musical of the Year' award. Three singers play Elvis at different stages of his life: young Tim Whitnall, Shaking Stevens as the teenager's idol, and P.J. Proby as Presley the man. Stevens is destined for stardom after his appearance in the musical, while Proby – who had once made 'demo' discs for Elvis – never quite fulfils his tremendous potential.

August 16, 1978. On the first anniversary of Elvis' death, Memphis marks the date with several special events: The Memphian Theatre which Elvis used to rent to watch movies shows a season of Presley films; Andy Warhol opens an exhibition of his painting, 'Elvis Forty-nine Times', at the Brooks Memorial Art Gallery; and, along with concerts featuring his music, a memorial service is held in the open on The Circle G Ranch. Despite a sudden strike by the local fire and police departments, thousands of fans come to the city from all over America and as far afield as Europe and Australia. In featuring the gathering, press and television are also quick to point out that in the past twelve months it is estimated Elvis' fans have spent more than $20 million on memorabilia!

September 1, 1978. A ten-day convention, 'Always Elvis', is staged by Colonel Parker at the Las Vegas Hilton which draws thousands of fans from all over the world to the venue which Elvis so often filled with song. Highlight of the event, which features the late singer's music and mementoes of his achievements, is a ceremony on September 8 when Priscilla Presley and Vernon Presley attend to unveil a larger-than-life bronze statue of Elvis placed at the entrance to the showroom – which is also dedicated to his memory. The statue, in typical pose with guitar and microphone, has been sculpted by Carl Romanelli. RCA Records also make a presentation to Vernon Presley of fifteen gold and platinum records in recognition of his son's record sales in the period of just one year *after* his death!

1979

February 11, 1979. Dick Clark, the famous Philadelphia disc jockey who had first brought Rock 'n' Roll to American teenagers and done much to promote Elvis' records in the early years, produces a made-for-television film, *Elvis,* aired on ABC-TV. Because Colonel Parker had refused Clark permission to use actual Presley recordings in his film, he casts Kurt Russell as Elvis with country singer, Ronnie McDowell dubbing his singing voice. Kurt's real-life father, Bing Russell, plays Vernon Presley, with Shelley Winters as Gladys Presley and Pat Hingle as Colonel Parker. Director John Carpenter produces a fascinating and authentic reconstruction of Elvis's incredible life, and such is the appeal of the film that, although it is shown opposite *Gone with the Wind* on CBS and Jack Nicholson's *One Flew Over the Cuckoo's Nest* on NBC, it receives a higher rating than the other two movies put together – 41 per cent of the audience.

June 26, 1979. After four years of ill-health – and the shattering blow of having lost his son as well as his first wife – Vernon Presley dies of heart failure. He had suffered a serious heart attack earlier in 1975 and the pressures of Elvis' final years undoubtedly undermined his health. He is buried in the Meditation Gardens in Graceland beside Gladys and their son.

August 17, 1979. Two years after his death, all the plans of Tupelo to mark the birthplace of its favourite son come to fruition with the opening of the Elvis Presley Park. This land, which surrounds the area of the simple wooden shack where Elvis was born, is turned into a picturesque attraction containing parkland, a community swimming pool and a Memorial Chapel which is dedicated on this day. Contributions from fans have helped create the Park, and the City of Tupelo also changes the name of the area around the now renovated shack to Presley Heights, while Old Saltillo Road becomes Elvis Presley Drive. The State of Mississippi also designates Elvis' birthplace as a Historical Monument. In Memphis, memorial services are held, a fibre-glass model of Eric Parks' statue of Elvis, which is to be erected in the city, is displayed, and the State University presents a series of seminars on the singer and his music. Shortly after this, the University of Tennessee begins the first formally accredited university level course on Elvis called 'Cultural Phenomenon of Elvis Presley: The Making of a Folk Hero.'

September 13, 1979. ABC Television's investigative programme, *20/20,* reveals the sensational news that it was drugs and not a heart attack that killed Elvis. Reporter Geraldo Rivera makes a convincing case for the singer's abuse of the drugs which were prescribed to him over many years for various complaints. Despite the widespread coverage of this revelation – and others still more sensational which follow in various newspapers and magazines – the loyalty of Elvis' fans to their dead hero remains undiminished.

1980

May 8, 1980. Death of Minnie Mae Presley, Elvis' paternal

grandmother, the oldest of his relatives and also the longest-lived. Nicknamed 'Dodger' by Elvis, she was a warm-hearted and humorous old lady who would never hear a bad word about her grandson. She is also buried in the grounds of Graceland where she had lived, alongside her family. With Minnie's death, little Lisa Marie becomes the sole heiress of Elvis' estate.

August 16, 1980. On the third anniversary of Elvis' death, Memphis adds to the honours heaped on its famous citizen by naming a portion of Beale Street – from where, of course, he drew some of his earliest musical inspiration – 'Elvis Presley Plaza'. The completed nine-foot high bronze statue by Eric Parks is also unveiled in the Plaza which is located just south of the downtown area. RCA also mark this day – which coincides with the 25th anniversary of their association with Elvis – by releasing an unprecedented eight-record LP album entitled simply, 'Elvis Aaron Presley', which mingles live performances and studio recordings, from 'Heartbreak Hotel' right through to the 1975 performance of 'Can't Help Falling in Love'.

December 23, 1980. Television personality David Frost presents an hour-long programme, *Elvis – He Touched Their Lives*, on British TV, which examines the enduring and widespread interest in Elvis by his fans even years after his death. Frost travels with 400 members of the Elvis Presley Fan Club of Great Britain on their annual pilgrimage to Memphis and provides an intriguing portrait of the phenomenon, sharing – as he later says – 'all the excitement, all the fresh emotion, and all the enthusiasm they felt for Elvis.'

1981

January 8, 1981. In the American Congress in Washington, Baltimore Representative Barbara Mikulski, introduces House Joint Resolution 488, 'authorising and requesting the President to issue a proclamation designating January 8, 1981, as "Elvis Presley Day".' Her motion is co-sponsored by other members of Congress from North Carolina to California. In Memphis, Sam Phillips pays his own personal tribute to the boy whom he helped start on the road to becoming a legend by seeking – and getting – permission from the Federal Communications Commission to change the call letters of his radio station to WLVS. Since then, not a day has passed without at least one Elvis record being broadcast from WLVS. The only sad note of this moment in time is the death of Felton Jarvis, producer of Elvis' records after Chet Atkins, shortly after completing the 'Guitar Man' LP on which he has re-mixed ten Presley recordings with new musical backing.

April 3, 1981. Release of *This Is Elvis*, Warner Brothers' authorised (by Colonel Parker) version of Elvis' life complete with still photography, early documentary film and TV footage, as well as interviews and concert performances. The film tries once more to explain the legend and the enigma of 'The King'. Actors and actresses play the central figures in the life story, interspersing the 'real' scenes – the highlights of these being some home movie shots of Elvis and Priscilla, extracts from the Sinatra and NBC Special shows in 1960 and 1968, and a sad but nonetheless moving monologue by Elvis at the very end of his career. Though reviews of the 101-minute movie written, produced and directed by Malcolm Leo and Andrew Solt, are varied, the reception by fans to this unique portrait of Elvis is universally good.

1982

June 7, 1982. After several years of delay, Graceland is finally opened to the public. Pressmen from all over the world cover this opening, Tony Frost of the London *Daily Mirror* writing, 'Since 1957 this 18-room mansion set in 13.4 acres of rolling green parkland has been one of the most closely guarded shrines in showbusiness. Outsiders have been kept at bay by armed security guards, electrical alarms, stone walls, closed circuit TV, and, at one stage, a posse of Karate-trained henchmen known as the "Memphis Mafia". But from tomorrow disciples can pay £2.50 for a stately-home style tour of the Presley mansion.' In the next twelve months, Frost adds, a million tourists are expected to cross the threshold of 3764 Elvis Presley Boulevard.

1983

October 27, 1983. Priscilla Presley, who has been pursuing a career in fashion and TV, lands a role in the enormously popular series, *Dallas,* and for the first time talks about her relationship with Elvis. Pouring scorn on many of the so-called 'revelations' about their marriage that have been made during the intervening years, she says: 'I loved Elvis. The day I married I was just someone very much in love who was going to be his wife – the rock star thing never meant anything to me. Nobody saw him as I did. He was very caring and very sensitive in many ways. But he was no angel. He had a lot of faults and a fierce, terrible temper. I know the fans want to hang on to the image of the perfect man. But it's not right. They saw him as a rock star, a movie idol, or just a crazy man. None of them saw Elvis as a real, complete human being – a combination of good and bad like everyone else.' Talking about how their marriage eventually failed, she goes on: 'I hate to remember that our marriage didn't turn out as we planned. People put him in a position he couldn't live up to. They just didn't understand that he wasn't a god, he was a man. And even if I had stayed with him, it would have ended the same way. I had done all I could for him. He had to do the rest himself and didn't. I couldn't have saved him.' Priscilla says that, despite feeling 'the weight of being Elvis' wife and of his memory still taking over my life' she plans to develop her acting career further, and to raise Lisa Marie, now a teenager, to as normal a life as possible. 'I was proud of Elvis then and I still am today,' she adds.

1984

January 8, 1984. Another side of Elvis' character is revealed by Larry Geller, a close friend for many years and the singer's spiritual adviser, while addressing a convention in London. He says that Elvis was deeply religious, meditated regularly and read the Bible every day. 'I helped him build up a library of more than 15,000 books on religion,' Geller says. 'He read them every day and took at least 200 books with him when he went on tour.' Revealing that he has written a book, *Elvis' Spiritual Journey,* Geller adds, 'I believe it is my mission to correct some of the many untruths that have been written about Elvis by people who hardly knew him.'

May 14, 1984. Fans are offered a further look into Elvis' life when the million dollar jet, the *Lisa Marie,* is put on public display at Memphis Airport. Features of the 'flying palace' are its incredible quadrophonic stereo system, bath with gold-plated taps and the huge, $15,000 bed.

1985

January 8, 1985. The Golden Anniversary of Elvis' birth. Had he lived, 'The King' would have celebrated his 50th birthday today – doubtless in traditional style at Graceland in company with his beautiful 16-year-old daughter. By now an elder statesman of the music business, this landmark in his life would surely have been marked by greetings from all over the world – and perhaps the decision at last to visit his worldwide assembly of fans? We shall never know – we can only speculate and *remember . . .*

Eyewitness to Presleymania

by Peter Dacre, *the first British journalist to interview Elvis*

When I flew from New York to Memphis, Tennessee, one day in October, 1956, I knew I was going to see a young man who was causing a stir with an uninhibited style of singing and a sex appeal that was causing screaming, weeping female havoc.

What I did not know was that Elvis Presley would revolutionise pop music and become a legend in his lifetime, a man hailed as 'The King'.

Of course, as in all revolutions, the time was ripe for change and the rise of a new leader. For the popular music scene of the early fifties was worn out and anaemic. We were still in the heyday of the ballad: Frank Sinatra singing 'Three Coins in the Fountain', Doris Day with 'Secret Love', Eddie Fisher warbling 'Oh, Mein Papa', Rosemary Clooney saying 'Hey, There,' Perry Como proclaiming 'No Other Love' and Frankie Laine telling us about 'A Woman In Love'.

In Britain we had Frankie Vaughan, David Whitfield, Ronnie Hilton, Anne Shelton and Ruby Murray. There was no definitive style of British pop, for mostly our home-grown stars sang 'cover' versions of American material.

True, there had been singers who caused screaming hysteria among female fans. There was the little-boy-lost appeal of Johnny Ray with his plaintive 'Cry' and the more robust, father-figure emotions aroused by our own Donald Peers. But there again the music was rooted in bland, synthetic Tin Pan Alley schmaltz.

The first notes of the new music came from Bill Haley and his Comets, with 'Rock Around the Clock'. Its impact in Britain was a warning of things to come. Bored with the musical pap they were being served, youngsters took to the emergent 'rock'n'roll' with such enthusiasm that there were near riots in the cinemas when the film *Rock Around the Clock* was shown, with dancing in the aisles and a bit of seat-wrecking as well.

But Haley's music was still merely a clever, synthetic music-business version of the black-rooted rock that was stirring in the Southern States.

And then along came Elvis Presley, wild, driving, raucous, and with a timbre to his voice that made him sound like a white negro.

So as I winged my way south that October day, a British reporter steeped in the conventional, show-business orien-tated music of the time, I was looking forward with great excitement – or at least as much excitement as a hard-headed reporter is allowed – to meeting and hearing Presley.

For me, it was more than an excursion into a world of new music: it was a foray into a new world and a new society – for I had never been to the South before. In Memphis, I found a new breed of people and a new style of living.

The novelty was not one way. A disc jockey I had contacted from New York, rushed me onto his programme, and while I was fascinated by the records he was playing – music you still did not hear in the North – he was equally fascinated by this strange-sounding character from 4,000 miles across the Atlantic.

But it was not until he drove me across the Tennessee–Mississippi border to Elvis' home town of Tupelo that the big impact came. Elvis was performing at an open-air concert at the Mississippi State Fair, which was spread over an expanse of fields on the borders of this small farming town.

The stage was surrounded by banked tiers of seats, packed with some 5,000 hysterical girls. Compared with the gigantic, 100,000 audiences for some latter-day pop groups, it was a modest-sized affair – but only in size. The atmosphere, the electric expectation in the hot Southern air, made me sense I was witnessing something extraordinary. Inside what was supposed to be Elvis' dressing room, a sizeable tent in a field at the side of the stage, I realised I was in the presence of a remarkable phenomenon.

The tent was a packed, brawling, oven-hot melée of people. As I talked to Elvis, we were surrounded by four armed state troopers, the Governor of Mississippi, the Mayor of Tupelo, radio reporters with thrusting micro-phones and photographers with flashing cameras.

In the centre of this chaos stood Elvis, relaxed and gum-chewing. He wore a blue velvet shirt, casually-open to reveal his bare chest, speckled black trousers and white shoes. On the fingers of his left hand were two gold rings, one with black sapphires, the other topped by a diamond horseshoe.

As I was not sure how much my paper would be interested in a pop star on the other side of the Atlantic – phenomenon or not – I had decided to try to put the interview on a serious level by addressing him as 'Mr'.

I had not bargained for the customary Southern politeness, for he addressed me as 'Sir'. It was an incongruous scene: two people addressing each other as 'Mr' and 'Sir' amid utter chaos!

'Mr Presley,' I said, 'are you aware of the sensation rock'n'roll music is causing in Britain?'

Elvis surveyed himself in the mirror. 'No, sir, I didn't know. I heard my records were going well over there, though.'

'Mr Presley,' I continued, 'can you explain the success of rock'n'roll and of your singing?'

Before he could reply a young girl broke through the

surrounding crowd, touched his three-inch sideburns and dashed out screaming: 'I touched him.'

Another girl thrust a lipstick into his hand and pleaded: 'Please, Elvis, autograph my back.'

Elvis obliged with what I must describe as a practised flourish.

'Mr Presley,' I persisted, 'about the success of rock'n'roll.'

'Oh, yes, sir,' he said. 'I wish I knew, sir. I've never been able to explain the reason for myself.'

'Why do you sing the way you do?' I asked.

'I like it that way,' Elvis replied with charming and pithy candour.

A burly state trooper thrust a pile of photographs between us. 'Sign these, Elvis,' he said.

Elvis began to sign away busily.

A young girl took a photograph, and almost fainted when he kissed her on the forehead loud and theatrically.

'Oh, Elvis, you are a darling,' she cried.

'Mr Presley,' I asked, 'what do you feel about all this adulation?'

To be fair, I suppose, Elvis could not be expected to understand the word. He chewed gum silently for a few seconds, tugged at his trousers and finally asked: 'All this what?'

'All these girls mobbing you like this,' I explained.

'I like it. I wouldn't be human if I didn't.'

I was beginning to warm to the simple honesty of the man.

The time for his performance was approaching, and from outside an announcer's voice boomed:

'We've got 500 National Guard and police here, so let's have no trouble. And please keep away from the stage. The last show, some of the girls got burnt from the stage lights, some of 'em got crushed – but none of 'em got Elvis.'

And then it was time for Elvis to be ushered on to the stage. For someone who had never seen him perform it was an amazing sight. He stood before the mike, loose-limbed, hips rolling. His lurching legs were straddled, both thighs undulating at once. His legs began flailing more frenetically and then suddenly he snapped them together like scissors.

As his performance continued he began playing with the microphone, which in 1956 was a stand-up instrument. He shook it about, straddled it and forced it down towards the stage, pointing outwards towards the imploring hands of his girl audience.

It was an incredibly erotic performance and it had a stunning effect on the girls. They screamed, banged on the stage, stretched out beseeching hands and tore their hair.

Photographers pushed on to the stage. Police joined them, but Elvis, seemingly impervious to their presence, kept on singing – and gyrating. One hysterical blonde managed to climb onto the stage and flung her arms around Presley. He kept on singing. Struggling and weeping, she was carried off.

Back, eventually, in the dressing room, the screaming cacophony continuing outside, I asked him the question which very few people have managed to put to him:

Elvis on stage in Tupelo in October 1956.

Giving it everything – another early shot of Elvis performing.

'Mr Presley, don't you think you sway about on stage too much while you're singing?'

He paused, wiping sweat from his forehead. 'Sir,' he replied, 'I don't reckon I do anything bad. I just move to the music on account of the way I feel. I hear it and I gotta move. I can't help it.

'People tell me: "You've got to stop squirming like a tadpole," but I'd sooner cut my throat than do anything vulgar. You've met my folks. They're respectable, God-fearing people. They wouldn't let me do anything vulgar.'

At the time I was not convinced, but the years proved that Elvis, brought up in the God-fearing Bible-belt, was remarkably strait-laced, and even prudish where women were concerned.

One impression I did get, though, was that while his performance was undeniably erotic, it was put over with lightly-teasing good-humour. There was an under-current of 'I'm-not-being-serious-girls'.

It was an element I have always thought was part of The Beatles' performance. And perhaps it is no coincidence that Presley and The Beatles have been the two greatest giants of them all.

Certainly Elvis revealed a sense of humour in conversation. When someone asked: 'Say, Elvis, will you have your picture taken with the Governor?' he put his arm around the Governor's shoulders and cracked: 'If I ever leave this business, I'll go into politics.'

'What will you run for?' someone asked.

'The city limits,' replied Elvis.

And it was clear that he remembered the hard-up days of his boyhood.

A young man came up to shake his hand, and Elvis slapped him on the back heartily. 'When we were kids, we used to slip into the Fair under the fence 'cause we had no money. But it's different now.'

I managed to lead him back to a comparatively quiet corner of the tent. 'Mr Presley,' I asked, 'what do you think of your success?'

'I don't ever think about it,' he replied, 'except sometimes when I wake up in the morning and say to myself: "Has this really happened to you?"'

Shortly afterwards he went off in his white Lincoln Continental. Even in those days, he already had four Cadillacs, a Messerchmitt runabout and a motor-cycle. In the years that followed, as the Presley legend grew, I sometimes wondered whether he continued to ask himself: 'Has this really happened to me?'

Or was the early humility replaced by the acceptance of someone who came to think he was born to be King?

Presleymania personified – a group of fans grab Elvis in mid-concert and for once he looks unconcerned!

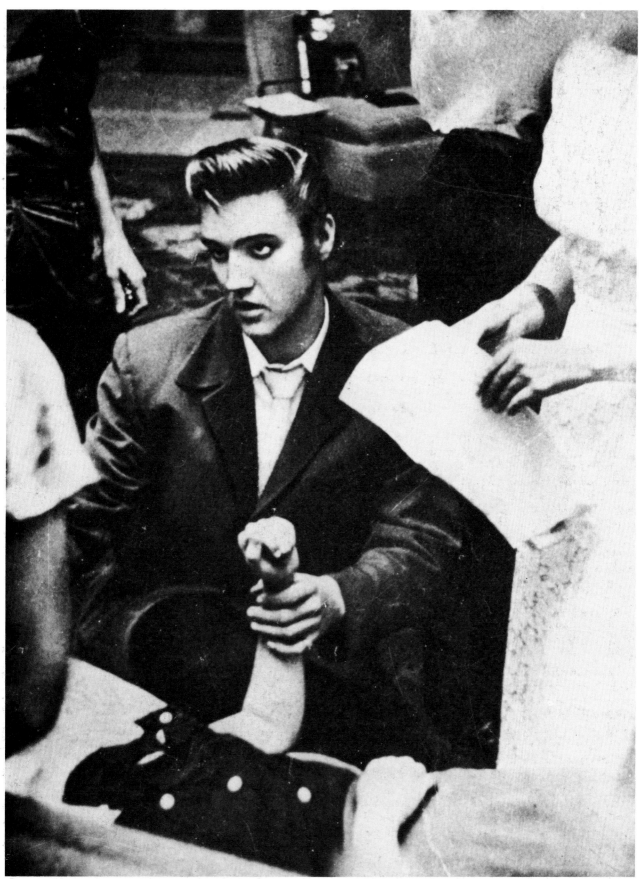

Elvis comforting a fan who has fainted at one of his early
concerts.

Recording Elvis

Chet Atkins, *Elvis' A & R man at RCA Records, discussing the singer at work with the author in 1963.*

I first met Elvis in 1954 when he played at The Grand Ole Opry in Nashville, the 'home' of country music. Even then he was someone you just couldn't miss because of his appearance. He had long hair and I can only describe the clothes he wore – black and pink – as lurid. Elvis also had the most extraordinary dark eyes – it looked just as if he was wearing make-up.

The date was September 24 and he had apparently driven all the way to Nashville from Memphis that day. With him were his group, Scotty Moore and Bill Black, as well as Sam Phillips who was recording him on his Sun label. Sam was just about to release Elvis' new single, 'Good Rockin' Tonight', and wanted to plug it on the show.

But Jim Denny, the manager of the Opry, refused point blank. He wanted Elvis to perform his current hit, 'That's All Right, Mama'. I believe he also wasn't too pleased that Elvis only had two other musicians with him – he seemed to think the sound Sam Phillips had got on the records was being made by at least a five- or six-piece band.

I suppose it's true that I was a bit more interested in Elvis than most of the other artists on the Opry that day because we had something in common. Like him, I'd first come to Nashville (back in 1943) hoping to get a spot on the show. Mind you, I just wanted to play guitar with one of the stars: I didn't see myself as a headliner.

I failed because I was too young and inexperienced, but it didn't put me off. After getting a lot of experience playing with small combos and working on radio stations in the South, I finally made it on the Opry in 1950. It was the answer to my prayers.

Like Elvis, too, I felt a bit let down when I first saw the old Ryman Auditorium in Nashville where the Opry was held. He said, 'Is this what I've been dreaming about all these years?' and I knew exactly what he meant because it was rather like an old barn.

It was while the rehearsals for the show were going on that I first spoke to Elvis. He came across and introduced himself – rather shyly and very politely. But he wasn't doing it for himself. He said his guitar player, Scotty Moore, was a big fan of my work and wanted to meet me!

Despite what some people have said and written, Elvis went over well with the live audience at the Opry that Saturday night – although most of them were older folk and young kids, rather than the teenagers he usually appealed to. But one person who wasn't impressed was Jim Denny. He told Elvis, 'We don't like that kind of music here. If I were you I'd go back to driving a truck.'

Elvis was pretty upset by that, I know, because it was much the same as happened to me.

It wasn't until January 1956 that I saw Elvis again, although I had heard what had happened to his career in the meantime. You couldn't open a newspaper or magazine in the South *without* knowing!

By then I was working for RCA Victor Records as the musical leader on their recording sessions in Nashville. The company had bought Elvis' contract from Sun and he was coming to cut his first sides for us. Before this, my boss, Steve Sholes, had me listen to all Elvis' Sun records. He also said he wanted me to play guitar on the first session.

It was an idea that appealed to me. I'd grown up on a farm in Tennessee and been much influenced by the music of the negro workers. It seemed to me that Elvis had fused their style of singing with that of country music in a quite unique way. It would be a real challenge to develop this fusion of two musical styles further still.

I remember that when Elvis came to our small studio on McGavock in Nashville he didn't talk much. I had sensed he was shy when we had met at the Opry and he didn't seem to have changed in the interim. I'm shy myself, so I knew the best thing would be just to let him get comfortable in his own way.

For a while Elvis just sat around, and then he started to sing some religious songs with The Jordanaires, whom we had brought in to provide the vocals. Gradually everyone relaxed.

Elvis played pretty good guitar, but he didn't utilise it all that much. Of course, he didn't need it, and on stage he used it more or less as a prop. But he could play that old Gibson well, and the piano, too.

I don't remember just how much guitar he played in the early sessions, other than just holding it and maybe strumming a chord now and then. But I do recall that he moved about so much that we had trouble with the microphones, and had to put a couple of other mikes alongside him to catch all the words he was singing. He just couldn't keep still!

That's how it all began. I played rhythm guitar and Scotty Moore played lead guitar. Elvis played rhythm sometimes and accompanied his singing. I think he could have been a great guitarist if he had worked at it.

Elvis had a fine musical ear, of course, and a great voice: much better than many people have given him credit for. And his feel for the kind of music that the kids would like was superb – because it was also what *he* liked!

The first song we actually completed on tape that first session was 'I Got A Woman'. Straight after that we did 'Heartbreak Hotel', though no one at the time realised how big it was going to be. After that, the rest is history.

Elvis at an early RCA recording session with Chet Atkins (*top left*), Steve Sholes (*left*), two members of the Jordanaires and with his back to the camera, Scotty Moore.

A simulated recording studio on the set of *Jailhouse Rock*,
with Scotty and Bill backing Elvis as usual.

When we were recording with Elvis we would often make a lot of tapes at the sessions. He always wanted to get the song just right, and would often say, 'I think I can do a little better,' and so off we would go again. He was always critical of himself, though, never of the other musicians.

In 1957, RCA made me chief A & R man in Nashville, and after that I only played on one more actual session with Elvis – in June 1958, just before he went into the Army. Hank Garland came in on guitar in place of Scotty Moore, and he was also in the session when we cut Elvis' first post-Army tapes in March 1960. From then on it was strictly the job of A & R man for me, arranging the sessions, booking the musicians, and so on.

By the sixties, Elvis had really matured musically, and I had very little to do on the sessions. I could just let Elvis get on with things in the studio and sit back and watch the tapes. Whatever he chose to do from the demos he was given – blues or rock, ballads or sacred music – he just had it all under control.

People often ask me about the 'Nashville Sound' they say Elvis has on some of his records. I think it is mostly a sound caused by Southern musicians and singers.

If you go into any area you will find that the musicians and singers have a certain style or a certain sound. Due to the good ears we have here we can distinguish that little difference that they have. And as to the musicians and singers who are from the South – and I include Elvis and myself – a lot of them were raised in poverty. They play by ear for the most part, and many of them learn to read out of necessity. But they still play with their ears, and if there is a 'Nashville Sound' I think that is what it is.

Really, though, the studios are the same and the same electronics exist everywhere. Technically, then, there is no 'Nashville Sound'. There may just be a 'Nashville Sound' in the styles or techniques of the musicians and the singers.

I have to admit, finally, that despite all the time we worked together, Elvis and I never talked that much. It really was a case of work, work, work, then quit and go home. In fact, I don't remember us having any real conversations to speak of.

But I always liked Elvis Presley and admired his talent very much.

An informal shot of Elvis on the drums at a recording session in Hollywood in 1957.

The King in Concert

Elvis' great live show triumphs as seen by his vocalist, Kathy Westmoreland

At the end of July 1969, after almost a decade of making only films and records, Elvis reappeared in public to begin what was to prove the last – and arguably most accomplished – period of his life: as the supreme live entertainer of the age.

As a legend in his own lifetime, Elvis, still only 34, was believed by many people to be beyond criticism; as a result of his domination of the entertainment scene and the astronomical sums of money he earned, he was now on a show business plateau of untouchability where it no longer mattered *what* he did. Journalists who had alternately damned and praised him, may well have felt that was the case – but Elvis' return to the exacting demands of the concert stage proved *he* did not.

There were those cynics, of course, who reacted to the announcement with their views that his voice had lost its unique edge, his wiggle had become more of a wobble, and his sexy good looks and lithe figure were decaying into flab. Indeed, they said that all those elements that had made him a teenage symbol who had radically affected the way people thought and lived were now just a memory, an echo of a personality as forever lost as the soul he had sung about all those years before in 'Heartbreak Hotel'.

But those fortunate enough to see him in person at a press conference announcing his opening at the giant new International Hotel in Las Vegas on July 31 – or in rehearsal – were instantly confounded. He was still devastatingly handsome – if anything, the passing years had refined his features – and his profile was now probably the most striking of any entertainer's since that of the great matinee idol, Rudolf Valentino. He looked slim, he dressed with consummate style, and carried himself with the athletic grace of a fit and healthy man. His voice, too, had all the old resonance when he spoke – and a hint of something else. It merely awaited the opening night to confirm that the dynamism was still there.

The reasons for the 'comeback' – as these self-same cynics chose to call the appearance of a man who had never really been away – were quickly made evident by Elvis himself.

'I've been wanting to perform again on the stage for the last nine years,' he said, 'but I had movie commitments and it's been building up inside of me since 1965 until the strain became intolerable. I got all het up about it, and I don't think I could have left it much longer. The time is just right.'

He referred to the intervening years with disarming candour. 'I wouldn't be being honest with you if I said I wasn't ashamed of some of the movies and some of the songs I've had to sing in them. I would like to say they were good,

but I can't. I've been extremely unhappy with that side of my career for some time. But how can you find 12 good songs for every film when you're making three films a year? I knew a lot of them were bad songs and they used to bother the heck out of me. But I had to do them. They fitted the situation.'

He smiled wryly and added, 'How can you enjoy it when you have to sing songs to the guy you've just punched up? No, I get more pleasure out of performing to an audience than any of the film songs have given me.'

There were inevitably comments passed by the journalists attending the press conference about his appearance after all the flurry of rumours in recent months. Again Elvis grinned widely. 'People keep telling me I look young,' he said. 'I don't know how I do it, either! It's true I got very heavy at one time when I was in all those movies, but I lose it quickly, you know!'

It was patently obvious from such exchanges that Elvis was in the highest of high spirits for his appearances in the International Hotel's huge showroom and, of course, the performances that he gave over the next four weeks are now part of legend – fans and reviewers alike overwhelmed and delighted at the return of 'The King'. For if anyone nursed doubts that he was still Number One, these shows swept aside such doubts with their mixture of showmanship, emotion and musical genius.

Elvis' concert dates and showroom appearances in the years which followed were triumphs of varying degrees, too, the only ultimate disappointment being that he did not take his mastery of live audiences beyond the shores of America to Europe, Britain, Australia, Japan and all the other points of the globe where his other millions of fans longed to see him – as, indeed, did he them. This said, his conquest of the most prestigious hall in America, Madison Square Gardens in New York in June 1972, remains one of his most outstanding achievements and possibly something he would have been unable to top anywhere else in the world. It was made all the more remarkable by being achieved in the city which had savaged him so unmercifully back in the 1950s. The people who had once derided him as a tuneless hillbilly now fell before the magic of his charisma and his incredible voice. The concerts remain vivid not only because of the live album recorded there, but also because of the unique insight we have of Elvis as a performer by someone who shared the stage with him, his back-up soprano vocalist, Kathy Westmoreland.

We also have Elvis himself on record giving another rare press conference before the four shows, spread over two days, which set New York alight. Again he handled the

104

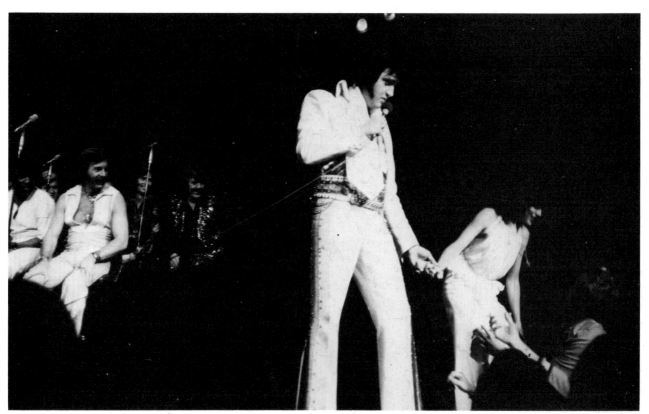

Elvis and Kathy Westmoreland take a bow together after yet another outstanding concert.

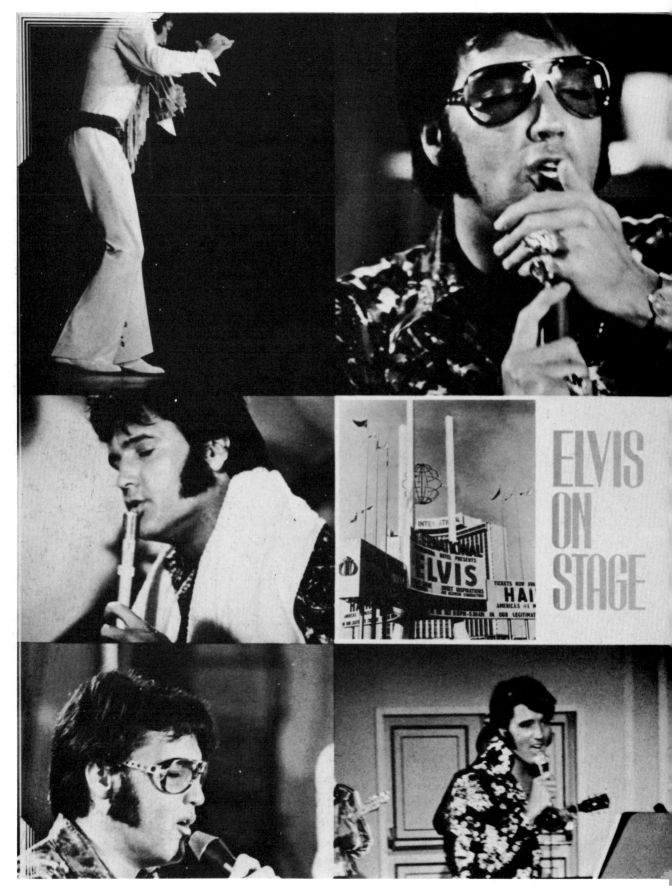

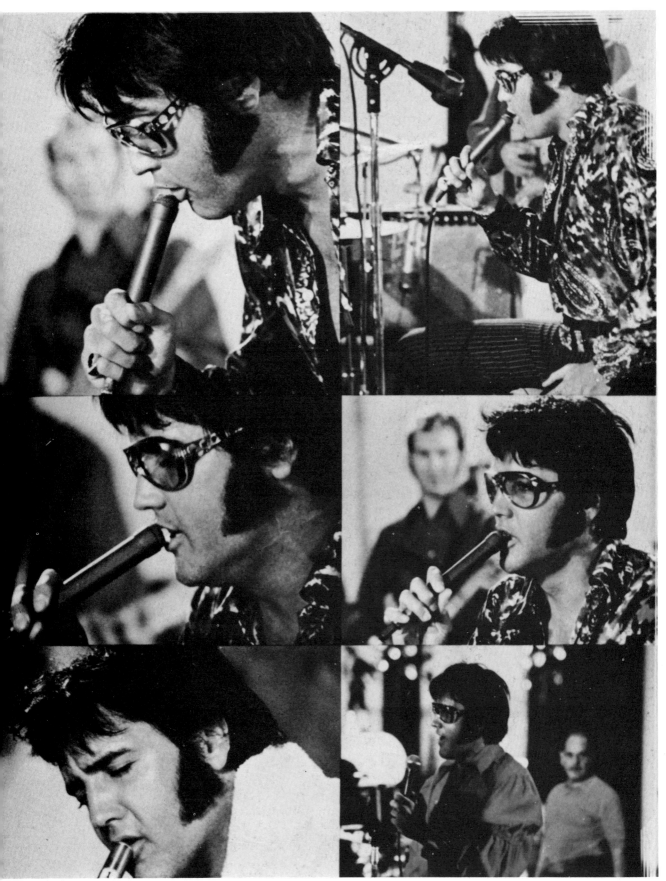

A montage of shots of Elvis in many moods during his performances in Las Vegas.

journalists with a skill which belied his humble origins and demonstrated a wholly captivating wit.

Did he think he was as good now as when he started, one gravel-voiced old veteran jibed.

'I'd like to think I've *improved*, sir,' Elvis replied. 'But I don't want to take anything away from the early hits. I'm not the least bit ashamed of "Hound Dog" or "Heartbreak Hotel".'

How had he managed to stay popular for so long, a female reporter enquired.

'I take Vitamin E,' he joked. 'No, actually honey, I don't know. I suppose I've just been fortunate – and I enjoy the business.'

Asked about his style of performance, Elvis said he thought he was 'tame to what some artists are doing now.' And he added, 'All *I* ever did was wiggle!'

Did the relentless screaming of his fans bother him?

'No sir,' he responded. 'I got used to them. I'd miss it now if it didn't happen. To me it's part of the business and I accept it.'

True to form, the screaming and roaring applause broke out in the cavernous interior of the Madison Square Gardens when Elvis' 30-piece band struck up on the evening of June 9 with his traditional entrance number, Richard Strauss' 'Also Sprach Zarathustra': the orchestral piece generally better known as the theme from the film, *2001: A Space Odyssey*.

Before Elvis appeared, a team of scarlet-jacketed security men rushed on to the huge rectangular stage, somehow heightening the excitement even further. Then came 'The King' himself – striding into view resplendent in a white suit flashing with silver sequins and gold appliqués, his shirt open across his chest and unbuttoned to the waist where a gold belt girdled his middle. A gold-lined cape hung from his shoulders, the collar faced in scarlet. Truly the entrance of a King of live entertainment.

With his very first number, 'That's All Right, Mama', Elvis transported his listeners back in time to the days when his career had been launched. A trip down memory lane, or a sly reminder of what the 'Big Apple' had once said of him? It mattered not, for everyone in that audience was now in his thrall.

And so on for fifty minutes more, twenty songs in all, each representing some highlight from the various periods of his career; the very titles of the numbers bringing memories tumbling back into the minds and hearts of those who were there: 'Proud Mary,' 'Never Been to Spain', 'You Don't Have To Say You Love Me', 'You've Lost That Loving Feeling', 'Polk Salad Annie', 'Love Me', 'All Shook Up', 'Heartbreak Hotel', a medley of 'Teddy Bear' and 'Don't Be Cruel', 'Love Me Tender', 'The Impossible Dream', 'Hound Dog', 'Suspicious Minds', 'For The Good Times', 'American Trilogy', 'Funny How Time Slips Away', 'I Can't Stop Loving You' and for a finale, 'Can't Help Falling In Love'.

Then Elvis left the stage with a wave. There were no encores, just the memory of a historic event. It was as if he existed only while he was on the stage. The disembodied voice of an announcer repeating, 'Elvis has left the building.

Thank you and goodnight,' seemed only to emphasise the fact.

Any of the critics who might have come to mock left instead to cheer. The *New York Post* compared his performance to that of a glittering diamond, while the *New York Times* was even more ecstatic. 'It was magnificent,' the paper reported. 'Of course Elvis sings his old favourites, doing a perfect impression of himself back in his blue-suede-shoes period. But the dumb seriousness of those days is now replaced with a mellow humour you can pick up on, even in the cheap seats. He understands perfectly the need to poke just a little fun at our own nostalgia. Surprisingly, dear, dated Elvis has moved more with the times than The Beatles or anyone else.'

New York magazine was even more analytical in its review. 'The performance he gave us was a spectacular triumph of insight into the mind of our mindless era. No demagogue of fact or legend has ever seen more keenly into the blackest depths of his followers, or grasped them in so many ways. He knows what ails and uplifts us, he rubs each of our dirtiest little secrets until it shines brightly in the dark, hollow arena of our souls.'

After all the mindless guff that had been written about Elvis himself over the years, such perceptive writing was welcome. Still more so are the 'up-close' observations of vocalist Kathy Westmoreland who by this time had already been his accompanist since 1970. When she had first gone to work with him, however, she had not been a fan and indeed thought his early songs were meaningless and his style rather bizarre.

'I wondered just how on earth I would fit in,' she said. 'I thought it would be funny being up there with him shaking his legs or swivelling his hips. But what would *I* do? How could a rock'n'roll singer use a soprano? And, I mean, my musical interests were totally opposite to his.'

Kathy had, though, worked with numerous top-line artists before, so she was not over-awed at what faced her. Indeed, she had really no idea just how big Elvis was with his audiences – though as soon as she appeared with him in Las Vegas for the first time and saw the hysteria he could generate she was absolutely amazed. But it was not this ability to drive fans wild that most impressed her about Elvis.

'The thing that really stood out for me was his musical ability,' she said. 'He did incredible things with his voice, and the feelings he had for the songs were quite different and more profound than any other artist I had ever heard. It was an emotional thing of a kind I had never experienced before.

'He also had an uncanny ear for anything in the orchestra. He'd hear things that no one else did. He would pick out something that no one else paid any attention to, something that the orchestra had lost. He knew exactly what was happening with every instrument. But he never made a fuss about mistakes, he just put them right and went on.'

Kathy recalled vividly her first days working with Elvis in Las Vegas at what was called his 'comeback'.

'He was absolute dynamite,' she said. 'Full of fun,

laughter and sheer energy. He was so full of energy that no one could keep up with him. I remember him saying how excited he was to be back in front of people again. Just the thought of people turning out in their thousands to see him seemed to excite him after all those years! He realised that for many people the performance was going to be one of the happiest moments of their lives.'

The antics of some of the 'happiest' people also stuck in Kathy's mind. 'Several girls just walked down a table,' she said, 'stepping on people's steaks, knocking over champagne, to get to him. I had never seen anything like that before. Then we went to the Veteran Coliseum in Phoenix and there was a bomb threat and the whole place had to be evacuated. There I was trying to think about what I should be doing and being distracted by the audience reaction to Elvis all the time!'

Elvis undoubtedly depended on his audiences, said Kathy. 'Their reassurance was what drove him on. He was very responsive to people and their feelings. Because you see he was actually very insecure and that helped him to create. He would either be trying to prove something to them or to himself, and out of that need he was able to create more than a person who was very secure. If he didn't do something right, or as well as he thought he could do it, he'd stop and do it over again in the middle of a song.'

Kathy believed that Elvis was what could be described as a 'generating force'. She explained, 'You would have to be dead not to feel what he was doing. He could get all those musicians from different musical backgrounds just to follow that feeling. He said to me very early on, "We're here to have a good time and make people happy – so don't worry about a thing. Do what you feel like doing." That helped me a lot. I felt free, and it was a new kind of freedom. Because for once there was nothing written out.

'Of course, you had to be with Elvis, but you were also free to improvise around that. Elvis himself got a great kick out of it when something new came up. It meant every number we did could be different, every show different. It made it all so exciting.

'Elvis taught me the joy of singing,' Kathy added, 'I had learnt, technically, how to sing, and I always sang with feeling. But he gave me a new spark. "If you're hurt," he once said to me, "let them see it in your song. If you're happy, let them feel it, too." He could see a unity of feeling and seeing as if it were all one thing.'

Kathy found Elvis to be a man of emotional extremes. One minute happy, the next sad. 'I remember once when we were rehearsing a happy song and having a really good time, he said, "Thank God for songs like that." And then right after that someone mentioned his mother. His face just changed instantly and you could almost see a tear in his eyes. And sometimes, when there had been talk about

Elvis 'cared so much about his audience' – as exemplified in this delightful moment with a very young fan . . .

something close to him, something emotional, he'd suddenly say, "Hey, that's enough of that!" and start laughing.'

Elvis had also told her that his happiest moments were on stage, Kathy added. 'That's all he ever really lives for. And yet there are so many pressures on him. And a person like him should only be concerned with singing. I honestly think he sometimes cares too much about his audiences and ignores himself.'

Prophetic words indeed: for the price Elvis ultimately paid for his devotion to you and me, his admirers, was of course his life. But we shall never forget him, and I venture to suggest that future generations will mark the one hundredth anniversary of his birth just as we mark the fiftieth.

His Melody will Linger On . . .

Sam Phillips, *the man who discovered Elvis, pays tribute in August 1977 to his achievements*

'It has been my personal policy to say very little about Elvis publicly before his death. However, I have been almost verbose about my beliefs in him privately throughout my association and acquaintance with him and I feel I can share these now.

'As the world knows, Elvis Presley was a shy young truck driver who just loved to sing. As fate would have it, he also just happened to walk in off the street to cut a record in my little Memphis studio in 1953.

'I wasn't there at the time, but my assistant Marion Keisker was impressed by his singing and kept a note of his name. A few months later I had a tune I wanted to record and no one to sing it. Marion reminded me of the singing truck driver and I called him in.

'There was no question in my mind – my business was to hear talent, no matter what state of polish it was in. Of course, none of us knew he was going to be that big, but the minute I heard the guy sing – it was an Ink Spot thing – he had a *unique* voice. Now there are very few things I am going to say are unique, that there's nothing else like them. But Elvis surely was.

'I called guitarist Scotty Moore and told him to get hold of bass player Bill Black. And I said, "I've got a young man and he's different." I told him and Bill to go by and work with Elvis a little. I said, "Now, he's really nervous and timid and extremely polite."

'And it took us quite a while. We worked off and on for about five to six months. I knew there were a lot of things we could have cut, but they weren't *different*. It was up to me to see the uniqueness of his talent and to go, hopefully, in the right direction with it.

'Now Elvis was aware that he had talent, but he had this modesty that was so genuine and almost overwhelming. Let me give you an example.

'You remember Clyde McPhatter? Elvis thought Clyde McPhatter had one of the greatest voices in the world. Well, one day we were going down to the Louisiana Hayride and we were singing in the car, Elvis, Scotty, Bill and I.

'Well, Bill Black couldn't carry a tune in a bucket, and Scotty was worse. So Elvis and I were the only good singers in the car. But we were talking about Clyde McPhatter, and he said, "You know, if I had a voice like that man, I'd never want for another thing."

'While we were working together at Sun he gained his confidence bit by bit. And not only did he evolve his style of rock 'n' roll with the three of us, but also picked up a love for the piano.

'He loved to sing and always wanted to play the guitar real good – though he never did learn to play that well – and he wanted to play the piano like Jerry Lee Lewis. Oh, he loved Jerry Lee's playing – he thought it was unbelievable.

'He didn't envy Jerry Lee or anything like that, but he did sit down and learn piano because he loved to hear Jerry Lee play so much. Man, he loved to play those old spiritual licks!

'Elvis' contributions to the great voids that existed during the fifties for a different approach to music for young people were monumental. He was the catalyst to the "sticking power" of this form of music that truly changed the approaches to music by making it freer and less pretentious for the whole world.

'With others like Jerry Lee, Carl Perkins, Johnny Cash and the many great black artists of the time, he helped pave a solid footing for all talent, both black and white, and gave a broader base for all aspiring young artists to spring from.

'Even after he became famous, Elvis never forgot how it had all started. He still liked to come back to the Sun studio or my house to sit and talk. He'd come by to see me, totally informally, never announcing the occasion. And we'd go off together and talk philosophy.

'I remember he called on the phone in 1968 from Las Vegas when he was about to return to live appearances. He said, "Mr Phillips, I just got to have you come out here. I'm scared to death. I got to have somebody I know, some friends, in the audience." I think Elvis was truly scared of being hurt, probably more than any person I know.

'The trouble was success like his is a vicious circle. You start out and you're so proud of your success and you say, "God, I'll do anything to stay on top." And then you find yourself saying, "Well, gosh, I know it's got to be over before too long and I've got to keep up this image. I'm very mortal, but I can't let the people know I'm mortal." But there's just no such thing as being an island unto yourself.

'I believe he needed help from the standpoint of forgetting all the money and all the fame. I'm not putting anybody down, but I am sure that after a long time Elvis just felt he didn't know how to do that. He became trapped in a lifestyle that kept him on a pedestal with the public but also kept him out of touch with reality.

'I really wish more people could have known him as a person. Elvis was a much, much deeper man and much more of a spiritual person than a lot of us may have thought.

'He also seemed uncomfortable with the way he was closed off from the pleasures of everyday life. A few years

Sam Phillips giving his discovery a few tips on the guitar!

back I talked to his doctor about this. I said, "This man, bless his heart, needs more than anybody I've ever seen to relax in his own home town at least. He needs to throw away the whole damn book and do whatever he damn well pleases. Let him be seen on the streets. It may take a while and a few guards at first . . ."

'I feel as fervently as I feel anything that he would be alive today if that had happened. You know, I think it's entirely possible to die of a broken heart . . . and I believe that was a contributing factor in what killed him.

'But we can all console ourselves that Elvis will never be forgotten. His feel for white and black country blues, along with his love for fundamental religious music, will stand him right at the top forever in the history of the basic changes that were so needed during this era of our music culture. These changes made life more meaningful and honest for us all.

'All of us are in his debt for the past, the present, and the future. His melody, believe me, will linger on!'

Early album sleeve for the fabulous group of songs that Elvis recorded for Sam Phillips' Sun label.

A sadly poignant shot of Elvis as always surrounded by
admirers at his last concert appearance in Cincinnati on
June 25 1977.

The Complete Elvis Song List A–Z

This listing contains the title of each song; the composer(s); the date of Elvis' *original* recording of the number; if released as a single; and as so much of Elvis' work was duplicated on various albums, the LP on which the song is most easily obtainable. (It should be noted that there are still a number of other songs that Elvis recorded during his career which were either featured in his films but never released on records, or else remain unreleased by RCA at the time of writing, and as such are therefore not listed hereunder.)

'A Big Hunk O'Love' (Schroeder & Wyche)	1958	single; LP *Elvis' Golden Records 2*
'A Boy Like Me, A Girl Like You' (Tepper & Bennett)	1962	LP *Girls! Girls! Girls!*
'Adam And Evil' (Wise & Star)	1966	LP *Spinout*
'A Dog's Life' (Wayne & Weisman)	1965	LP *Paradise, Hawaiian Style*
'A Fool Such As I' (Trader)	1958	single; LP *Elvis' Golden Records 2*
'After Loving You' (Miller & Lantz)	1969	LP *Clambake*
'A House That Has Everything' (Tepper & Bennett)	1967	LP *Clambake*
'Ain't That Loving You Baby' (Otis & Hunter)	1958	single; LP *Elvis' Golden Records 4*
'A Little Bit Of Green' (Arnold, Morrow & Martin)	1969	LP *Back In Memphis*
'A Little Less Conversation' (Strange & Davis)	1968	single
'All I Needed Was The Rain' (Weisman & Wayne)	1967	LP *Elvis Sings Flaming Star*
'All Shook Up' (Blackwell & Presley)	1957	single; LP *Pure Gold*
'All That I Am' (Tepper & Bennett)	1966	single; LP *Spinout*
'Almost' (Kaye & Weisman)	1968	LP *Let's Be Friends*
'Almost Always True' (Wise & Weisman)	1961	LP *Blue Hawaii*
'Almost In Love' (Bonfa & Starr)	1968	single; LP *Almost In Love*
'Aloha-Oe' (Trad. arranged Presley)	1961	LP *Blue Hawaii*
'Always On My Mind' (Carson, James & Christopher)	1972	single; LP *Separate Ways*
'Amazing Grace' (Trad. arranged Presley)	1971	LP *He Touched Me*
'An American Trilogy' (Trad. arranged Newbury)	1972	single; LP *Elvis At Madison Square Gardens*
'A Mess Of Blues' (Pomus & Schuman)	1960	single; LP *Elvis' Golden Records 4*
'Am I Ready' (Tepper & Bennett)	1966	LP *Burning Love*
'And I Love You So' (McLean)	1975	LP *Today*
'And The Grass Won't Pay No Mind' (Diamond)	1969	LP *Back In Memphis*
'An Evening Prayer' (Battersby & Gabriel)	1971	LP *He Touched Me*
'Angel' (Tepper & Bennett)	1961	LP *C'mon Everybody*
'Animal Instinct' (Giant, Baum & Kaye)	1965	LP *Harum Scarum*
'Any Day Now' (Hilliard & Bacharach)	1969	single; LP *From Elvis In Memphis*
'Anyone' (Benjamin, Marcus & Dejesus)	1963	LP *Kissin' Cousins*
'Anyplace Is Paradise' (Thomas)	1956	LP *Elvis*
'Anything That's Part Of You' (Robertson)	1961	single; LP *Elvis' Golden Records 3*
'Any Way You Want Me' (Schroeder & Owens)	1956	single
'Are You Lonesome Tonight?' (Turk & Handman)	1960	single; LP *Elvis In Concert*
'Are You Sincere?' (Walker)	1973	LP *Raised On Rock*
'Ask Me' (Modugno, Giant, Baum & Kaye)	1963	single
'As Long As I Have You' (Wise & Weisman)	1958	LP *King Creole*
'A Thing Called Love' (Hubbard)	1970	LP *He Touched Me*
'A Whistling Tune' (Edwards & David)	1961	EP *Kid Galahad*
'A World Of Our Own' (Giant, Baum & Kaye)	1962	LP *It Happened At The World's Fair*
'Baby, I Don't Care' (Leiber & Stoller)	1957	LP *A Date With Elvis*
'Baby If You'll Give Me All Of Your Love' (Byers)	1966	LP *Double Trouble*
'Baby Let's Play House' (Gunter)	1955	single; LP *The Sun Sessions*
'Baby What Do You Want Me To Do?' (Reed)	1968	LP *Elvis – A Legendary Performer 2*
'Barefoot Ballad' (Fuller & Morris)	1963	LP *Kissin' Cousins*

113

'Beach Boy Blues' (Tepper & Bennett)	1961	LP *Blue Hawaii*
'Beach Shack' (Giant, Baum & Kaye)	1966	LP *Spinout*
'Because Of Love' (Batchelor & Roberts)	1962	LP *Girls! Girls! Girls!*
'Beginner's Luck' (Tepper & Bennett)	1965	LP *Frankie & Johnny*
'Beyond The Bend' (Weisman, Wise & Fuller)	1962	LP *It Happened At The World's Fair*
'Beyond The Reef' (Pitman)	1966	LP *How Great Thou Art*
'Big Boots' (Wayne & Edwards)	1960	LP *G.I. Blues*
'Big Boss Man' (Smith & Dixon)	1967	single; LP *Clambake*
'Big Love, Big Heartache' (Fuller, Morris & Hendrix)	1964	LP *Roustabout*
'Bitter They Are, Harder They Fall' (Gatlin)	1976	LP *From Elvis Presley Boulevard*
'Blueberry Hill' (Lewis, Stock & Rose)	1956	LP *Loving You*
'Blue Christmas' (Heyes & Johnson)	1957	single; LP *Elvis' Christmas Album*
'Blue Eyes Crying In The Rain' (Rose)	1976	LP *From Elvis Presley Boulevard*
'Blue Hawaii' (Robin & Rainger)	1961	LP *Blue Hawaii*
'Blue Moon' (Rogers & Hart)	1954	single; LP *The Sun Sessions*
'Blue Moon Of Kentucky' (Monroe)	1954	single; LP *The Sun Sessions*
'Blue River' (Evans & Tobias)	1963	single; LP *Double Trouble*
'Blue Suede Shoes' (Perkins)	1956	single; LP *Elvis – A Legendary Performer 1*
'Bosom Of Abraham' (Johnson, McFadden & Brooks)	1971	LP *He Touched Me*
'Bossa Nova Baby' (Leiber & Stoller)	1963	single; LP *Fun In Acapulco*
'Bridge Over Troubled Water' (Simon)	1970	LP *Elvis – That's The Way It Is*
'Bringing It Back' (Gordon)	1975	single; LP *Today*
'Britches' (Tepper & Bennett)	1960	EP *Elvis Sings Flaming Star*
'Bullfighter Was A Lady' (Tepper & Bennett)	1963	LP *Fun In Acapulco*
'Burning Love' (Linde)	1972	single; LP *Aloha From Hawaii*
'By And By' (Trad. arranged Presley)	1966	LP *How Great Thou Art*
'Cane And A High Starched Collar' (Tepper & Bennett)	1960	LP *Elvis – A Legendary Performer 2*
'Can't Help Falling In Love' (Peretti, Creatore & Weiss)	1961	single; LP *Blue Hawaii*
'Carny Town' (Wise & Starr)	1964	LP *Roustabout*
'Catchin' On Fast' (Giant, Baum & Kaye)	1963	LP *Kissin' Cousins*
'Change Of Habit' (Kaye & Weisman)	1969	LP *Let's Be Friends*
'Charro' (Davis & Strange)	1968	single; LP *Almost In Love*
'Chesay' (Karger, Weisman & Wayne)	1965	LP *Frankie & Johnny*
'Cindy, Cindy' (Kaye, Weisman & Fuller)	1970	LP *Love Letters From Elvis*
'City By Night' (Giant, Baum & Kaye)	1966	LP *Double Trouble*
'Clambake' (Weisman & Wayne)	1967	LP *Clambake*
'Clean Up Your Own Backyard' (Strange & Davis)	1968	single; LP *Almost In Love*
'C'Mon Everybody' (Byers)	1963	LP *C'Mon Everybody*
'Come Along' (Hess)	1965	LP *Frankie & Johnny*
'Come What May' (Tableporter)	1966	single
'Confidence' (Tepper & Bennett)	1967	LP *Clambake*
'Cotton Candy Land' (Batchelor & Roberts)	1962	LP *It Happened At The World's Fair*
'Could I Fall In Love?' (Starr)	1966	LP *Double Trouble*
'Crawfish' (Wise & Weisman)	1958	LP *King Creole*
'Cross My Heart And Hope To Die' (Wayne & Weisman)	1964	LP *Girl Happy*
'Crying In The Chapel' (Glenn)	1960	single; LP *How Great Thou Art*
'Danny Boy' (Weatherly)	1976	LP *From Elvis Presley Boulevard*
'Datin'' (Wise & Starr)	1965	LP *Paradise, Hawaiian Style*
'Devil In Disguise' (Giant, Baum & Kaye)	1963	single; LP *Elvis' Golden Records 4*
'Didja Ever' (Wayne & Edwards)	1960	LP *G.I. Blues*
'Dirty, Dirty Feeling' (Leiber & Stoller)	1960	EP *Tickle Me*
'Dixieland Rock' (Schroeder & Frank)	1958	LP *King Creole*
'Doin' The Best I Can' (Pomus & Schuman)	1960	LP *G.I. Blues*
'Doncha' Think It's Time?' (Otis & Dixon)	1958	single; LP *Elvis' Golden Records 2*
'Do Not Disturb' (Giant, Baum & Kaye)	1964	LP *Girl Happy*
'Don't' (Leiber & Stoller)	1957	single; LP *Elvis' Golden Records 2*
'Don't Ask Me Why' (Wise & Weisman)	1958	single; LP *King Creole*
'Don't Be Cruel' (Blackwell & Presley)	1956	single; LP *Pure Gold*
'Don't Cry Daddy' (Scott & Davis)	1969	single; LP *Worldwide 50 Gold Award Hits 1*
'Don't Leave Me Now' (Schroeder & Weisman)	1957	LP *Loving You*
'Don't Think Twice' (Dylan)	1971	LP *Elvis*
'Do The Clam' (Wayne, Weisman & Fuller)	1964	single; LP *Girl Happy*
'Do The Vega' (Giant, Baum & Kaye)	1963	LP *Elvis Sings Flaming Star*

Song	Year	Release
'Double Trouble' (Pomus & Schuman)	1966	LP *Double Trouble*
'Down By The Riverside' (Trad. arranged Giant, Baum & Kaye)	1956	LP *Frankie & Johnny*
'Down In The Alley' (Stone)	1966	LP *Spinout*
'Do You Know Who I Am?' (Russell)	1969	single
'Drums Of The Island' (Tepper & Bennett)	1965	LP *Paradise, Hawaiian Style*
'Early Morning Rain' (Lightfoot)	1971	LP *Elvis Now*
'Earth Boy' (Tepper & Bennett)	1962	LP *Girls! Girls! Girls!*
'Easy Come, Easy Go' (Weisman & Wayne)	1966	LP *C'Mon Everybody*
(Such An) 'Easy Question' (Blackwell & Scott)	1962	single; LP *Pot Luck*
'Echoes Of Love' (Roberts & McMains)	1963	LP *Kissin' Cousins*
'Edge Of Reality' (Giant, Baum & Kaye)	1968	single; LP *Almost In Love*
'El Toro' (Giant, Baum & Kaye)	1963	LP *Fun In Acapulco*
'Elvis – His First & Only Press Conference'	1972	LP
'Elvis Presley's Newsreel Interview'	1958	LP *Worldwide 50 Gold Award Hits 1*
'Everybody Come Aboard' (Giant, Baum & Kaye)	1965	LP *Frankie & Johnny*
'Eyes Of Texas' (Sinclair)	1963	LP *Viva Las Vegas*
'Faded Love' (Wills)	1970	LP *Elvis Country*
'Fair's Moving On' (Flett & Fletcher)	1969	single; LP *Back In Memphis*
'Fairy Tale' (Pointer)	1975	LP *Today*
'Fame And Fortune' (Wise & Weisman)	1960	single; LP *Elvis' Golden Records 3*
'Farther Along' (Trad. arranged Presley)	1966	LP *How Great Thou Art*
'Fever' (Davenport & Cooley)	1960	LP *Elvis Is Back!*
'Finders Keepers, Losers Weepers' (Jones)	1963	LP *Elvis For Everyone*
'Find Out What's Happening' (Crutchfield)	1973	LP *Raised On Rock*
'First In Line' (Schroeder & Weisman)	1956	LP *Elvis*
'First Noel' (Trad. arranged Presley)	1971	LP *Elvis Sings The Wonderful World of Christmas*
'First Time Ever I Saw Your Face' (MacColl)	1971	single
'Five Sleepy Heads' (Tepper & Bennett)	1967	LP *Speedway*
'Flaming Star' (Wayne & Edwards)	1960	LP *Elvis Sings Flaming Star*
'Flip, Flop And Fly' (Turner)	1956	LP *Elvis Live In Memphis*
'Follow That Dream' (Wise & Weisman)	1961	LP *C'Mon Everybody*
'Fool' (Sigman & Last)	1972	single; LP *Elvis*
'Fools Fall In Love' (Leiber & Stoller)	1966	single; LP *I Got Lucky*
'Fools Rush In' (Bloom & Mercer)	1971	LP *Elvis Now*
'Forget Me Never' (Wise & Weisman)	1960	LP *Elvis For Everyone*
'For Old Times' Sake' (White)	1973	single; LP *Raised On Rock*
'For The Good Times' (Kristofferson)	1972	LP *Elvis At Madison Square Gardens*
'For The Heart' (Linde)	1976	single; LP *From Elvis Presley Boulevard*
'For The Millionth And The Last Time' (Tepper & Bennett)	1961	LP *Elvis For Everyone*
'Fort Lauderdale Chamber of Commerce' (Tepper & Bennett)	1964	LP *Girl Happy*
'Fountain of Love' (Giant & Lewis)	1962	LP *Pot Luck*
'Frankfurt Special' (Wayne & Edwards)	1960	LP *G.I. Blues*
'Frankie & Johnny' (Gottlied, Karger & Weisman)	1965	single; LP *Frankie & Johnny*
'From A Jack To A King' (Miller)	1969	LP *From Memphis To Vegas*
'Fun In Acapulco' (Weisman & Wayne)	1963	LP *Fun In Acapulco*
'Funny How Time Slips Away' (Nelson)	1969	LP *Elvis Country*
'Gentle On My Mind' (Hartford)	1969	LP *From Elvis In Memphis*
'Gently' (Wizell & Lisbona)	1961	LP *Something For Everybody*
'G.I. Blues' (Tepper & Bennett)	1960	LP *G.I. Blues*
'Girl Happy' (Pomus & Meade)	1964	LP *Girl Happy*
'Girl I Never Loved' (Starr)	1967	LP *Clambake*
'Girl Next Door Went A'Walking' (Rice & Wayne)	1960	LP *Elvis Is Back!*
'Girl Of Mine' (Reed & Mason)	1973	LP *Raised On Rock*
'Girl Of My Best Friend' (Ross & Bobrick)	1960	LP *Elvis Is Back!*
'Girls! Girls! Girls!' (Leiber & Stoller)	1962	LP *Girls! Girls! Girls!*
'Give Me The Right' (Wise & Blagman)	1961	LP *Something For Everybody*
'Go East, Young Man' (Giant, Baum & Kaye)	1965	LP *Harum Scarum*
'Goin' Home' (Byers)	1967	LP *Speedway*
'Golden Coins' (Giant, Baum & Kaye)	1965	LP *Harum Scarum*
'Gonna Get Back Home Somehow' (Pomus & Schuman)	1962	LP *Pot Luck*
'Good Luck Charm' (Schroeder & Gold)	1961	single; LP *Elvis' Golden Records 3*
'Good Rockin' Tonight' (Brown)	1954	single; LP *The Sun Sessions*

The raw young talent – 'Heartbreak Hotel' (1956).

The new movie star – 'Love Me Tender' (1956).   117

'Good Time Charlie's Got The Blues' (O'Keefe)	1973	LP *Good Times*
'Got A Lot Of Livin' To Do' (Schroeder & Weisman)	1957	LP *Loving You*
'Got My Mojo Working' (Foster)	1970	LP *Love Letters From Elvis*
'Green Green Grass Of Home' (Putman)	1975	LP *Today*
'Greenback Dollar, Watch And Chain' (Harris)	1957	single
'Guadalajara' (Guizar)	1963	LP *Fun In Acapulco*
'Guitar Man' (Reed)	1967	single; LP *Clambake*
'Happy Ending' (Weisman & Wayne)	1962	LP *It Happened At The World's Fair*
'Harbour Lights' (Kennedy & Williams)	1954	LP *Elvis – A Legendary Performer 2*
'Hard Headed Woman' (Demetrius)	1958	single; LP *King Creole*
'Hard Knocks' (Byers)	1964	LP *Roustabout*
'Hard Luck' (Weisman & Wayne)	1965	LP *Frankie & Johnny*
'Harum Holiday' (Andreoli & Poncia)	1965	LP *Harum Scarum*
'Have A Happy' (Weisman, Kaye & Fuller)	1969	LP *Let's Be Friends*
'Have I Told You Lately That I Love You?' (Weisman)	1957	LP *Loving You*
'Hawaiian Sunset' (Tepper & Bennett)	1961	LP *Blue Hawaii*
'Hawaiian Wedding Song' (King, Hoffman & Manning)	1961	LP *Blue Hawaii*
'Heartbreak Hotel' (Axton & Durden)	1956	single; LP *Elvis' Golden Records 1*
'Heart Of Rome' (Stephens, Blakley & Howard)	1970	single; LP *Love Letters From Elvis*
'He Is My Everything' (Frazier)	1971	LP *He Touched Me*
'He Knows Just What I Need' (Lister)	1960	LP *His Hand In Mine*
'He'll Have To Go' (Allison)	1971	LP *Moody Blue*
'Help Me' (Gatlin)	1973	single; LP *Elvis In Memphis*
'Help Me Make It Through The Night' (Kristofferson)	1971	LP *Elvis Now*
'Here Comes Santa Claus' (Autry, Haldeman & Melka)	1957	LP *Elvis' Christmas Album*
'He's Your Uncle, Not Your Dad' (Wayne & Weisman)	1967	LP *Speedway*
'He Touched Me' (Gaither)	1971	LP *He Touched Me*
'Hey, Hey, Hey' (Byers)	1967	LP *Clambake*
'Hey, Jude' (Lennon & McCartney)	1969	LP *Elvis Now*
'Hey, Little Girl' (Byers)	1965	LP *Harum Scarum*
'High Heel Sneakers' (Higgenbottom)	1967	single
'His Hand In Mine' (Lister)	1960	single; LP *His Hand In Mine*
(Marie's The Name) 'His Latest Flame' (Pomus & Schuman)	1961	single; LP *Elvis' Golden Records 3*
'Holly Leaves And Christmas Trees' (West & Spreen)	1971	LP *Elvis Sings The Wonderful World of Christmas*
'Home Is Where The Heart Is' (Edwards & David)	1961	LP *I Got Lucky*
'Hot Dog' (Leiber & Stoller)	1957	LP *Loving You*
'Hound Dog' (Leiber & Stoller)	1956	single; LP *Elvis' Golden Records 1*
'House Of Sand' (Giant, Baum & Kaye)	1965	LP *Paradise, Hawaiian Style*
'How Can You Lose What You Never Had?' (Weisman & Wayne)	1967	LP *Clambake*
'How Do You Think I Feel?' (Walker & Pierce)	1956	LP *Elvis*
'How Great Thou Art' (Hine)	1966	single; LP *How Great Thou Art*
'How's The World Treating You?' (Atkins & Bryant)	1956	LP *Elvis*
'How The Web Was Woven' (Westlake & Most)	1970	LP *Elvis – That's The Way It Is*
'How Would You Like To Be?' (Raleigh & Barman)	1962	single; LP *It Happened At The World's Fair*
'Hurt' (Craine & Jacobs)	1976	single; LP *From Elvis Presley Boulevard*
'I Beg Of You' (McCoy & Owens)	1957	single; LP *Elvis' Golden Records 2*
'I Believe' (Drake, Graham, Shirl & Stillman)	1957	LP *Elvis' Christmas Album*
'I Believe In The Man In The Sky' (Howard)	1960	single; LP *His Hand In Mine*
'I Can Help' (Swan)	1975	LP *Today*
'I Can't Stop Loving You' (Gibson)	1969	LP *From Memphis To Vegas*
'I Don't Care If The Sun Don't Shine' (David)	1954	single; LP *The Sun Sessions*
'I Don't Wanna Be Tied' (Giant, Baum & Kaye)	1962	LP *Girls! Girls! Girls!*
'I Don't Want To' (Torre & Spielman)	1962	LP *Girls! Girls! Girls!*
'I Feel So Bad' (Willis)	1961	single; LP *Elvis' Golden Records 3*
'I Feel That I've Known You Forever' (Pomus & Jeffries)	1962	LP *Pot Luck*
'If Every Day Was Like Christmas' (West)	1966	single; LP *Elvis' Christmas Album*
'If I Can Dream' (Brown)	1968	single; LP *Elvis – A Legendary Performer 2*
'If I Get Home On Christmas Day' (McCauley)	1971	LP *Elvis Sings The Wonderful World of Christmas*
'If I'm A Fool' (Kesler)	1969	LP *Let's Be Friends*
'If I Were You' (Nelson)	1970	LP *That's The Way It Is*
'I Forgot To Remember To Forget' (Kesler & Feathers)	1955	single; LP *The Sun Sessions*
'If That Isn't Love' (Rambo)	1973	LP *Good Times*
'If The Lord Wasn't Walking By My Side' (Slaughter)	1966	LP *How Great Thou Art*

'If We Never Meet Again' (Brumley)	1960 LP *His Hand In Mine*
'If You Don't Come Back' (Leiber & Stoller)	1973 LP *Raised On Rock*
'If You Love Me' (Rostill)	1977 LP *Elvis In Concert*
'If You Talk In Your Sleep' (West & Christopher)	1973 single; LP *Promised Land*
'If You Think I Don't Need You' (West & Cooper)	1963 LP *I Got Lucky*
'I Got A Feelin' In My Body' (Linde)	1973 LP *Good Times*
'I Got A Woman' (Charles)	1956 single; LP *Pure Gold*
'I Got Lucky' (Fuller, Weisman & Wise)	1961 LP *I Got Lucky*
'I Got Stung' (Schroeder & Hill)	1958 single; LP *Elvis' Golden Records 2*
'I Gotta Know' (Evans & Williams)	1960 single; LP *Elvis' Golden Records 3*
'I, John' (Johnson, McFadden & Brooks)	1971 LP *He Touched Me*
'I Just Can't Help Believing' (Mann & Weill)	1970 LP *Elvis – That's The Way It Is*
'I'll Be Back' (Wayne & Weisman)	1966 LP *Spinout*
'I'll Be Home For Christmas' (Kent, Gammon & Ram)	1957 LP *Elvis' Christmas Album*
'I'll Be Home On Christmas Day' (Jarrett)	1971 LP *Elvis Sings The Wonderful World of Christmas*
'I'll Be There (If Ever You Want Me)' (Gabbard & Price)	1971 LP *Let's Be Friends*
'I'll Hold You In My Heart' (Arnold, Horton & Dilbeck)	1969 LP *From Elvis In Memphis*
'I'll Never Fall In Love Again' (Donegan & Currie)	1976 LP *From Elvis Presley Boulevard*
'I'll Never Know' (Karger, Wayne & Weisman)	1970 LP *Love Letters From Elvis*
'I'll Never Let You Go, Little Darling' (Wakely)	1954 single; LP *The Sun Sessions*
'I'll Remember You' (Lee)	1966 LP *Spinout*
'I'll Take Love' (Fuller & Barkan)	1966 LP *C'Mon Everybody*
'I'll Take You Home Again, Kathleen' (Trad. arranged Presley)	1971 LP *Elvis*
'I Love Only One Girl' (Tepper & Bennett)	1966 LP *Double Trouble*
'I Love You Because' (Payne)	1954 single; LP *The Sun Sessions*
'I'm Comin' Home' (Rich)	1961 LP *Something For Everybody*
'I'm Counting On You' (Robertson)	1956 single; LP *Elvis Presley*
'I Met Her Today' (Robertson & Blair)	1961 LP *Elvis For Everyone*
'I'm Falling In Love Tonight' (Robertson)	1962 LP *It Happened At The World's Fair*
'I'm Gonna Sit Right Down And Cry Over You' (Thomas & Biggs)	1956 single; LP *Elvis Presley*
'I'm Gonna Walk Dem Golden Stairs' (Trad. arranged Presley)	1960 LP *His Hand In Mine*
'I Miss You' (Sumner)	1973 LP *Raised On Rock*
'I'm Leaving' (Jarrett & Charles)	1971 single
'I'm Left, You're Right, She's Gone' (Kesler & Taylor)	1955 single; LP *The Sun Sessions*
'I'm Movin' On' (Snow)	1969 LP *From Elvis In Memphis*
'Impossible Dream' (Leigh & Darion)	1972 LP *Elvis At Madison Square Gardens*
'I'm Not The Marrying Kind' (David & Edwards)	1961 LP *C'Mon Everybody*
'I'm So Lonesome I Could Cry' (Williams)	1973 LP *Aloha From Hawaii*
'I'm Yours' (Robertson & Blair)	1961 single; LP *Pot Luck*
'Indescribably Blue' (Glenn)	1966 single; LP *Elvis' Golden Records 4*
'I Need Somebody To Lean On' (Pomus & Schuman)	1963 LP *I Got Lucky*
'I Need Your Love Tonight' (Wayne & Reichner)	1958 single; LP *Elvis' Golden Records 2*
'I Need You So' (Hunter)	1957 LP *Loving You*
'Inherit The Wind' (Rabbitt)	1969 LP *From Memphis To Vegas*
'In My Father's House' (Hanks)	1960 LP *His Hand In Mine*
'In My Way' (Wise & Weisman)	1960 LP *Elvis For Everyone*
'In The Garden' (Miles)	1966 LP *How Great Thou Art*
'In The Ghetto' (Davis)	1969 single; LP *Pure Gold*
'In Your Arms' (Schroeder & Gold)	1961 LP *Something For Everybody*
'I Really Don't Want To Know' (Robertson & Barnes)	1970 single; LP *Elvis Country*
'I Slipped, I Stumbled, I Fell' (Wise & Weisman)	1960 LP *Something For Everybody*
'Is It So Strange?' (Young)	1957 LP *A Date With Elvis*
'Island of Love (Kauai)' (Tepper & Bennett)	1961 LP *Blue Hawaii*
'It Ain't No Big Thing' (Merritt, Joy & Hall)	1970 LP *Love Letters From Elvis*
'It Feels So Right' (Wise & Weisman)	1960 single; LP *Elvis Is Back!*
'I Think I'm Gonna Like It Here' (Robertson & Blair)	1963 LP *Fun In Acapulco*
'It Hurts Me' (Byers)	1968 single; LP *Elvis' Golden Records 4*
'It Keeps Right On A-Hurting' (Tillotson)	1969 LP *From Elvis In Memphis*
'Ito Eats' (Tepper & Bennett)	1961 LP *Blue Hawaii*
'It Is No Secret (What God Can Do)' (Hamblen)	1957 LP *Elvis' Christmas Album*
'It's A Matter of Time' (Westlake)	1972 single; LP *Burning Love*
'It's A Sin' (Rose & Turner)	1961 LP *Something For Everybody*
'It's A Wonderful World' (Tepper & Bennett)	1964 LP *Roustabout*
'It's Carnival Time' (Weisman & Wayne)	1964 LP *Roustabout*
'It's Impossible' (Wayne & Manzanero)	1972 LP *Pure Gold*
'It's Midnight' (Wheeler & Chesnut)	1973 single; LP *Promised Land*

'It's Now Or Never' (Schroeder & Gold)   1960   single; LP *Elvis' Golden Records 3*
'It's Only Love' (James & Tyrell)   1971   single
'It's Over' (Rodgers)   1972   LP *Aloha From Hawaii*
'It's Still Here' (Hunter)   1971   LP *Elvis*
'It's Your Baby, You Rock It' (Milete & Fowler)   1970   LP *Elvis Country*
'It Won't Be Long' (Weisman & Wayne)   1966   LP *Double Trouble*
'It Won't Seem Like Christmas' (Balthrop)   1971   LP *Elvis Sings the Wonderful World of Christmas*
'I've Got A Thing About You, Baby' (White)   1973   single; LP *Good Times*
'I've Got Confidence' (Crouch)   1971   LP *He Touched Me*
'I've Got To Find My Baby' (Byers)   1964   LP *Girl Happy*
'I've Lost You' (Howard & Blaickley)   1970   single; LP *Elvis – That's The Way It Is*
'I Want To Be Free' (Leiber & Stoller)   1957   LP *A Date With Elvis*
'I Want You, I Need You, I Love You' (Mysels & Kosloff)   1956   single; LP *Elvis' Golden Records 2*
'I Want You With Me' (Harris)   1961   LP *Something For Everybody*
'I Was Born About Ten Thousand Years Ago' (Trad. arranged Presley)   1970   LP *Elvis Now*
'I Washed My Hands In Muddy Waters' (Babcock)   1970   LP *Elvis Country*
'I Was The One' (Schroeder, Demetrius, Blair & Peppers)   1956   single; LP *Worldwide Gold Award Hits 2*
'I Will Be Home Again' (Benjamin, Leveen & Singer)   1956   LP *Elvis Is Back!*
'I Will Be True' (Hunter)   1971   LP *Elvis*

'Jailhouse Rock' (Leiber & Stoller)   1957   single; LP *Pure Gold*
'Jesus Knows What I Need' (Maine)   1961   LP *His Hand In Mine*
'Johnny B. Goode' (Berry)   1969   LP *From Memphis To Vegas*
'Joshua Fit The Battle' (Trad. arranged Presley)   1960   single; LP *His Hand In Mine*
'Judy' (Redell)   1961   single; LP *Something For Everybody*
'Just A Little Bit' (Thornton, Brown, Bass & Washington)   1973   LP *Raised On Rock*
'Just Because' (Shelton & Robin)   1954   single; LP *The Sun Sessions*
'Just Call Me Lonesome' (Griffin)   1967   LP *Clambake*
'Just For Old Times' Sake' (Tepper & Bennett)   1962   LP *Pot Luck*
'Just Pretend' (Flett & Fletcher)   1970   LP *Elvis – That's The Way It Is*
'Just Tell Her Jim Said Hello' (Leiber & Stoller)   1962   single; LP *Elvis' Golden Records 4*

'Kentucky Rain' (Rabbitt & Heard)   1969   single; LP *Pure Gold*
'King Creole' (Leiber & Stoller)   1958   LP *King Creole*
'King Of The Whole Wide World' (Batchelor & Roberts)   1961   LP *C'Mon Everybody*
'Kismet' (Tepper & Bennett)   1965   LP *Harum Scarum*
'Kissin' Cousins' (Wise & Starr)   1963   LP *Kissin' Cousins*
'Kiss Me Quick' (Pomus & Schuman)   1961   single; LP *Pot Luck*
'Known Only To Him' (Hamblen)   1960   single; LP *His Hand In Mine*
'Ku-u-i-po' (Peretti, Creatore & Weiss)   1961   LP *Blue Hawaii*

'Last Farewell' (Whittaker & Webster)   1976   LP *From Elvis Presley Boulevard*
'Lawdy, Miss Clawdy' (Price)   1956   single; LP *Elvis Live In Memphis*
'Lead Me, Guide Me' (Akers)   1971   LP *He Touched Me*
'Let It Be Me' (Curtis, Delanoe & Becaud)   1970   LP *On Stage*
'Let Me' (Maton & Presley)   1956   LP *Worldwide Gold Award Hits 2*
'Let Me Be There' (Rostill)   1974   LP *Elvis Live In Memphis*
'Let's Be Friends' (Arnold, Morrow & Martin)   1969   LP *Let's Be Friends*
'Let's Forget About The Stars' (Owens)   1969   LP *Let's Be Friends*
'Let Us Pray' (Weisman & Kaye)   1969   LP *You'll Never Walk Alone*
'Let Yourself Go' (Byers)   1968   single; LP *Speedway*
'Life' (Milete)   1970   single; LP *Love Letters From Elvis*
'Like A Baby' (Stone)   1960   LP *Elvis Is Back!*
'Little Cabin On The Hill' (Monroe & Flatt)   1970   LP *Elvis Country*
'Little Darling' (Williams)   1977   LP *Moody Blue*
'Little Egypt' (Leiber & Stoller)   1964   LP *Roustabout*
'Little Sister' (Pomus & Schuman)   1961   single; LP *Elvis' Golden Records 3*
'Lonely Man' (Benjamin & Marcus)   1960   single; LP *Elvis' Golden Records 4*
'Lonesome Cowboy' (Tepper & Bennett)   1957   LP *Loving You*
'Long Black Limousine' (Stowall & George)   1969   LP *From Elvis In Memphis*
'Long Legged Girl' (McFarland & Scott)   1966   single; LP *Double Trouble*
(It's A) 'Long Lonely Highway' (Pomus & Schuman)   1963   single; LP *Kissin' Cousins*
'Long Tall Sally' (Johnson, Penniman & Blackwell)   1956   LP *Elvis*
'Look Out Broadway' (Wise & Starr)   1965   LP *Frankie & Johnny*
'Love Coming Down' (Chesnut)   1976   LP *From Elvis Presley Boulevard*

120

'Love Letters' (Young & Heyman)	1966	single; LP *Elvis' Golden Records 4*
'Love Machine' (Nelson, Burch & Taylor)	1966	LP *I Got Lucky*
'Love Me' (Leiber & Stoller)	1956	LP *Elvis*
'Love Me, Love The Life I Lead' (Macauley & Greenaway)	1971	LP *Elvis*
'Love Me Tender' (Matson & Presley)	1956	single; LP *Pure Gold*
'Love Me Tonight' (Robertson)	1963	LP *Fun In Acapulco*
'Lover Doll' (Wayne & Silver)	1958	single; LP *King Creole*
'Love Song Of The Year' (Christian)	1973	LP *Promised Land*
'Loving Arms' (Jans)	1973	LP *Good Times*
'Loving You' (Leiber & Stoller)	1957	single; LP *Loving You*
'Make Me Know It' (Blackwell)	1960	LP *Elvis Is Back!*
'Make The World Go Away' (Cochran)	1970	LP *Elvis Country*
'Mama' (O'Curran & Brooks)	1962	LP *Let's Be Friends*
(Your) 'Mama Don't Dance' (Loggins & Mesina)	1974	LP *Elvis Live In Memphis*
'Mama Liked The Roses' (Christopher)	1969	single; LP *Elvis' Christmas Album*
'Mansion Over The Hilltop' (Stamphill)	1960	LP *His Hand In Mine*
'Marguerita' (Robertson)	1963	LP *Fun In Acapulco*
'Mary In The Morning' (Cymbal & Rashkow)	1970	LP *Elvis – That's The Way It Is*
'Meanest Girl In Town' (Byers)	1964	LP *Girl Happy*
'Mean Woman Blues' (Demetrius)	1957	LP *Loving You*
'Memories' (Strange & Davis)	1968	single; LP *Elvis – TV Special*
'Memphis, Tennessee' (Berry)	1963	LP *Elvis For Everyone*
'Merry Christmas, Baby' (Baxter & Moore)	1971	single; LP *Elvis Sings The Wonderful World of Christmas*
'Mexico' (Tepper & Bennett)	1963	LP *Fun In Acapulco*
'Milkcow Blues Boogie' (Arnold)	1954	single; LP *The Sun Sessions*
'Milky White Way' (Trad. arranged Presley)	1960	single; LP *His Hand In Mine*
'Mine' (Tepper & Bennett)	1967	LP *Speedway*
'Miracle Of The Rosary' (Denson)	1971	LP *Elvis Now*
'Mirage' (Giant, Baum & Kaye)	1965	LP *Harum Scarum*
'Money Honey' (Stone)	1956	single; LP *Elvis Presley*
'Moody Blue' (James)	1976	LP *Moody Blue*
'Moonlight Swim' (Dee & Weisman)	1961	LP *Blue Hawaii*
'Mr Songman' (Sumner)	1973	single; LP *Promised Land*
'My Babe' (Dixon)	1969	LP *From Memphis To Vegas*
'My Baby Is Gone' (Kesler & Tayler)	1955	LP *Good Rockin' Tonight*
'My Baby Left Me' (Crudup)	1956	single; LP *Worldwide Gold Award Hits 2*
'My Boy' (Martin & Coulter)	1973	single; LP *Good Times*
'My Desert Serenade' (Gelber)	1965	LP *Harum Scarum*
'My Little Friend' (Milete)	1969	single; LP *Almost In Love*
'Mystery Train' (Philips & Parker)	1955	single; LP *The Sun Sessions*
'My Way' (Anka, Reyoux & François)	1973	LP *Aloha From Hawaii*
'My Wish Came True' (Hunter)	1957	single; LP *Elvis' Golden Records 2*
'Never Again' (Wheeler & Chesnut)	1976	LP *From Elvis Presley Boulevard*
'Never Been To Spain' (Axton)	1972	LP *Elvis At Madison Square Gardens*
'Never Ending' (Kaye & Springer)	1963	single; LP *Double Trouble*
'Never Say Yes' (Pomus & Schuman)	1966	LP *Spinout*
'New Orleans' (Tepper & Bennett)	1958	LP *King Creole*
'Next Stop Is Love' (Evans & Parnes)	1970	single; LP *Elvis – That's The Way It Is*
'Night Life' (Giant, Baum & Kaye)	1963	LP *Elvis Sings Flaming Star*
'Night Rider' (Pomus & Schuman)	1961	LP *Pot Luck*
'No More' (Robertson & Blair)	1961	LP *Blue Hawaii*
(There's) 'No Room To Rhumba In A Sports Car' (Wise & Manning)	1963	LP *Fun In Acapulco*
'Nothingsville' (Strange & Davis)	1968	LP *Elvis – TV Special*
'O Come All Ye Faithful' (Trad. arranged Presley)	1971	single; LP *Elvis Sings the Wonderful World of Christmas*
'Oh Little Town Of Bethlehem' (Trad. arranged Presley)	1957	single; LP *Elvis' Christmas Album*
'Old MacDonald' (Starr)	1966	LP *Double Trouble*
'Old Shep' (Foley)	1956	LP *Elvis*
'On A Snowy Christmas Eve' (Gelber)	1971	LP *Elvis Sings The Wonderful World of Christmas*
'Once Is Enough' (Tepper & Bennett)	1963	LP *Kissin' Cousins*
'One Boy, Two Little Girls' (Giant, Baum & Kaye)	1963	LP *Kissin' Cousins*
'One Broken Heart For Sale' (Blackwell & Scott)	1962	single; LP *It Happened At The World's Fair*
'One Night' (Bartholomew & King)	1957	single; LP *Elvis' Golden Records 2*

'One Sided Love Affair' (Cambell)	1956	single; LP *Elvis Presley*
'One Track Heart' (Giant, Baum & Kaye)	1964	LP *Roustabout*
'Only Believe' (Rader)	1970	single; LP *Love Letters From Elvis*
'Only The Strong Survive' (Gamble, Huff & Buthey)	1969	LP *From Elvis In Memphis*
'Padre' (Larue, Webster & Romans)	1971	LP *Elvis*
'Paradise, Hawaiian Style' (Giant, Baum & Kaye)	1965	LP *Paradise, Hawaiian Style*
'Paralysed' (Blackwell & Presley)	1956	LP *Elvis*
'Party' (Robinson)	1957	LP *Loving You*
'Pat Hernon Interviews Elvis'	1958	LP *Elvis – A Legendary Performer 1*
'Patch It Up' (Rabbitt & Bourke)	1970	single; LP *Elvis – That's The Way It Is*
(There'll Be) 'Peace In The Valley' (Dorsey)	1957	LP *Elvis' Christmas Album*
'Petunia, The Gardener's Daughter' (Tepper & Bennett)	1965	LP *Frankie & Johnny*
'Pieces Of My Life' (Seals)	1975	single; LP *Today*
'Playing For Keeps' (Kesler)	1956	single; LP *Worldwide 50 Gold Award Hits 1*
'Please Don't Drag That String Around' (Blackwell & Scott)	1963	single; LP *Elvis' Golden Records 4*
'Please Don't Stop Loving Me' (Byers)	1965	single; LP *Frankie & Johnny*
'Pledging My Love' (Washington & Robey)	1976	LP *Moody Blue*
'Pocketful of Rainbows' (Wise & Weisman)	1960	LP *G.I. Blues*
'Poison Ivy League' (Giant, Baum & Kaye)	1964	LP *Roustabout*
'Polk Salad Annie' (White)	1970	LP *Elvis At Madison Square Gardens*
'Poor Boy' (Martin & Coulter)	1956	LP *Worldwide Gold Award Hits 2*
'Power Of My Love' (Giant, Baum & Kaye)	1969	LP *From Elvis In Memphis*
'Press Interview With Elvis'	1958	LP *Worldwide 50 Gold Award Hits 1*
'Promised Land' (Berry)	1973	single; LP *Promised Land*
'Proud Mary' (Fogerty)	1970	LP *Elvis At Madison Square Gardens*
'Puppet On A String' (Tepper & Bennett)	1964	single; LP *Worldwide Gold Award Hits 2*
'Put The Blame On Me' (Twomey, Wise & Blagman)	1961	LP *Something For Everybody*
'Put Your Hand In The Hand' (MacLellan)	1971	LP *Elvis Now*
'Queenie Wahine's Papaya' (Giant, Baum & Kaye)	1965	LP *Paradise, Hawaiian Style*
'Rags To Riches' (Adler & Ross)	1970	single
'Raised On Rock' (James)	1973	single; LP *Raised On Rock*
'Reach Out To Jesus' (Carmichael)	1971	LP *He Touched Me*
'Ready Teddy' (Blackwell & Marascalco)	1956	LP *Elvis*
'Reconsider, Baby' (Fulson)	1960	LP *Elvis Is Back!*
'Relax' (Tepper & Bennett)	1962	LP *It Happened At The World's Fair*
'Release Me' (Miller & Stevenson)	1970	LP *February 1970 – On Stage*
'Return To Sender' (Blackwell & Scott)	1962	single; LP *Worldwide 50 Gold Award Hits 1*
'Riding The Rainbow' (Weisman & Wise)	1961	LP *I Got Lucky*
'Rip It Up' (Blackwell & Marascalco)	1956	LP *Elvis*
'Rock-A-Hula Baby' (Wise, Weisman & Fuller)	1961	single; LP *Blue Hawaii*
'Roustabout' (Giant, Baum & Kaye)	1964	LP *Roustabout*
'Rubberneckin'' (Jones & Warren)	1969	single; LP *Almost In Love*
'Runaway' (Shannon & Croak)	1969	LP *February 1970 – On Stage*
'Run On' (Trad. arranged Presley)	1966	LP *How Great Thou Art*
'Sand Castles' (Goldberg & Hess)	1965	LP *Paradise, Hawaiian Style*
'Santa, Bring My Baby Back' (Schroeder & Demetrius)	1957	LP *Elvis' Christmas Album*
'Santa Claus Is Back In Town' (Leiber & Stoller)	1957	single; LP *Elvis' Christmas Album*
'Santa Lucia' (Trad. arranged Presley)	1963	LP *Elvis For Everyone*
'Saved' (Leiber & Stoller)	1968	LP *Elvis – TV Special*
'Scratch My Back, Then I'll Scratch Yours' (Giant, Baum & Kaye)	1965	LP *Paradise, Hawaiian Style*
'See See Rider' (C. C. Rider) (Trad. arranged Presley)	1970	LP *Elvis Live In Memphis*
'Seeing Is Believing' (West & Spreen)	1971	LP *He Touched Me*
'Sentimental Me' (Cassin & Morehead)	1961	LP *Something For Everybody*
'Separate Ways' (West & Mainegra)	1972	single; LP *Separate Ways*
'Shake A Hand' (Morris)	1975	LP *Today*
'Shake, Rattle And Roll' (Calboun)	1956	single; LP *For LP Fans Only*
'Shake That Tambourine' (Giant, Baum & Kaye)	1965	LP *Harum Scarum*
'She's A Machine' (Byers)	1966	LP *Elvis Sings Flaming Star*
'She's Not You' (Pomus, Stoller & Leiber)	1962	single; LP *Elvis Golden Records 3*
'She Thinks I Still Care' (Lee)	1976	LP *Moody Blue*

'She Wears My Ring' (Bryant)	1973	LP *Good Times*
'Shoppin' Around' (Tepper, Bennett & Schroeder)	1960	LP *G.I. Blues*
'Shout It Out' (Giant, Baum & Kaye)	1965	LP *Frankie & Johnny*
'Silent Night' (Mohr & Gruber)	1957	LP *Elvis' Christmas Album*
'Silver Bells' (Evans & Livingston)	1971	LP *Elvis Sings The Wonderful World of Christmas*
'Singing Tree' (Owens & Solberg)	1967	LP *Clambake*
'Sing, You Children' (Nelson & Burch)	1966	LP *You'll Never Walk Alone*
'Slicin' Sand' (Tepper & Bennett)	1961	LP *Blue Hawaii*
'Slowly But Surely' (Wayne & Weisman)	1963	LP *Fun In Acapulco*
'Smokey Mountain Boy' (Rosenblatt & Milrose)	1963	LP *Kissin' Cousins*
'Smorgasbord' (Tepper & Bennett)	1966	LP *Spinout*
'Snowbird' (MacLellan)	1970	LP *Elvis Country*
'So Close, Yet So Far From Paradise' (Byers)	1965	LP *Harum Scarum*
'So Glad You're Mine' (Crudup)	1956	LP *Elvis*
'So High' (Trad. arranged Presley)	1966	LP *How Great Thou Art*
'Soldier Boy' (Jones & Williams Jnr.)	1960	LP *Elvis Is Back!*
'Solitaire' (Sedaka & Cody)	1976	LP *From Elvis Presley Boulevard*
'Somebody Bigger Than You And I' (Large, Heath & Burk)	1966	LP *How Great Thou Art*
'Something' (Harrison)	1973	LP *Aloha From Hawaii*
'Something Blue' (Evans & Byron)	1962	LP *Pot Luck*
'Song Of The Shrimp' (Tepper & Bennett)	1962	LP *Girls! Girls! Girls!*
'Sound Advice' (Giant, Baum & Kaye)	1961	LP *Elvis For Everyone*
'Sound Of Your City' (Adams)	1970	single
'Spanish Eyes' (Kaempfert, Singleton & Snyder)	1973	LP *Good Times*
'Speedway' (Glazer & Schlaks)	1967	LP *Speedway*
'Spinout' (Wayne, Weisman & Fuller)	1966	single; LP *Spinout*
'Spring Fever' (Giant, Baum & Kaye)	1964	LP *Girl Happy*
'Stand By Me' (Trad. arranged Presley)	1966	LP *How Great Thou Art*
'Starting Today' (Robertson)	1961	LP *Something For Everybody*
'Startin' Tonight' (Rosenblatt & Millrose)	1964	LP *Girl Happy*
'Stay Away' (Tepper & Bennett)	1967	single; LP *Almost In Love*
'Stay Away Joe' (Weisman & Wayne)	1967	LP *Let's Be Friends*
'Steadfast, Loyal And True' (Leiber & Stoller)	1958	LP *King Creole*
'Steamroller Blues' (Taylor)	1973	single; LP *Aloha From Hawaii*
'Steppin' Out Of Line' (Wise, Weisman & Fuller)	1961	LP *Pot Luck*
'Stop, Look And Listen' (Byers)	1966	LP *Spinout*
'Stop Where You Are' (Giant, Baum & Kaye)	1965	LP *Paradise, Hawaiian Style*
'Stranger In My Own Home Town' (Mayfield)	1969	LP *Back In Memphis*
'Stranger In The Crowd' (Scott)	1970	LP *Elvis – That's The Way It Is*
'Stuck On You' (Schroeder & McFarland)	1960	single; LP *Elvis' Golden Records 3*
'Such A Night' (Chase)	1960	single; LP *Elvis Is Back!*
'Summer Kisses, Winter Tears' (Wise, Weisman & Lloyd)	1960	LP *Elvis For Everyone*
'Suppose' (Dee & Goehring)	1967	LP *Speedway*
'Surrender' (Pomus & Schuman)	1960	single; LP *Elvis' Golden Records 3*
'Susan When She Tried' (Reid)	1975	LP *Today*
'Suspicion' (Pomus & Schuman)	1962	single; LP *Pot Luck*
'Suspicious Minds' (James)	1969	single; LP *Aloha From Hawaii*
'Sweet Angeline' (Arnold, Martin & Morrow)	1973	LP *Raised On Rock*
'Sweet Caroline' (Diamond)	1970	LP *February 1970 – On Stage*
'Swing Low, Sweet Chariot' (Trad. arranged Presley)	1960	single; LP *His Hand In Mine*
'Sylvia' (Stephens & Reed)	1970	LP *Elvis Now*
'Take Good Care Of Her' (Warren & Kent)	1973	single; LP *Good Times*
'Take Me To The Fair' (Tepper & Bennett)	1962	LP *It Happened At The World's Fair*
'Take My Hand, Precious Lord' (Dorsey)	1957	LP *You'll Never Walk Alone*
'Talk About The Good Times' (Hubbard)	1973	LP *Good Times*
'(Let Me Be Your) Teddy Bear' (Mann & Loewe)	1957	single; LP *Elvis' Golden Records 1*
'Tell Me Why' (Turner)	1957	single; LP *Worldwide Gold Award Hits 2*
'Tender Feeling' (Giant, Baum & Kaye)	1963	LP *Kissin' Cousins*
'Thanks To The Rolling Sea' (Batchelor & Roberts)	1962	LP *Girls! Girls! Girls!*
'That's All Right, Mama' (Crudup)	1954	single; LP *The Sun Sessions*
'That's Someone You Never Forget' (West & Presley)	1961	single; LP *Pot Luck*
'That's When Your Heartaches Begin' (Fisher, Hill & Raskin)	1957	single; LP *Elvis' Golden Records 1*
'The Fool' (Ford)	1970	LP *Elvis Country*
'There Ain't Nothing Like A Song' (Byers & Johnston)	1967	LP *Speedway*

The versatile singer – 'Fun In Acapulco' (1963).

The television star – 'Guitar Man' (NBC 1968).

'There Goes My Everything' (Frazier)	1970	single; LP *Elvis Country*
'There Is No God But God' (Kenny)	1971	LP *He Touched Me*
'There's A Brand New Day On The Horizon' (Byers)	1964	LP *Roustabout*
'There's A Honky Tonk Angel' (Seal & Rice)	1973	LP *Promised Land*
'There's Always Me' (Robertson)	1961	single; LP *Something For Everybody*
'There's A Fire Down Below' (Scheff)	1976	LP *Moody Blue*
'There's Gold In The Mountains' (Giant, Baum & Kaye)	1963	LP *Kissin' Cousins*
'There Is So Much World To See' (Tepper & Weisman)	1966	LP *Double Trouble*
'They Remind Me Too Much Of You' (Robertson)	1962	single; LP *Worldwide Gold Award Hits 2*
'Thinking About You' (Baty)	1973	single; LP *Promised Land*
'This Is Living' (Weisman & Wise)	1961	LP *C'Mon Everybody*
'This Is My Heaven' (Giant, Baum & Kaye)	1965	LP *Paradise, Hawaiian Style*
'This Is Our Dance' (Reed & Stephens)	1970	LP *Love Letters From Elvis*
'This Is The Story' (Arnold, Morrow & Martin)	1969	LP *Back In Memphis*
'Three Corn Patches' (Leiber & Stoller)	1973	LP *Raised On Rock*
'Thrill Of Your Love' (Kesler)	1960	LP *Elvis Is Back!*
'Tiger Man' (Lewis & Burns)	1968	LP *From Memphis To Vegas*
'Today, Tomorrow And Forever' (Giant, Baum & Kaye)	1963	LP *C'Mon Everybody*
'Tomorrow Is A Long Time' (Dylan)	1966	LP *Spinout*
'Tomorrow Never Comes' (Tubb & Bond)	1970	LP *Elvis Country*
'Tomorrow Night' (Coslow & Grosz)	1955	LP *Elvis For Everyone*
'Tonight Is So Right For Love' (Wayne & Silver)	1960	LP *G.I. Blues*
'Tonight's All Right For Love' (Wayne, Silver & Lilly)	1960	LP *Elvis – A Legendary Performer 1*
'Too Much' (Rosenberg & Weisman)	1956	single; LP *Elvis' Golden Records 2*
'Too Much Monkey Business' (Berry)	1968	LP *Elvis Sings Flaming Star*
'Treat Me Nice' (Leiber & Stoller)	1957	single; LP *Elvis' Golden Records 1*
'T-r-o-u-b-l-e' (Chesnut)	1975	single, LP *Today*
'Trouble' (Leiber & Stoller)	1958	LP *King Creole*
'True Love' (Porter)	1957	LP *Loving You*
'True Love Travels On A Gravel Road' (Owen & Frazier)	1969	LP *From Elvis In Memphis*
'Trying To Get To You' (Singleton & McCoy)	1955	single; LP *The Sun Sessions*
'Tutti Frutti' (La Bostrie & Penniman)	1956	single; LP *Elvis Presley*
'Twenty Days And Twenty Nights' (Weisman & Westlake)	1970	LP *Elvis – That's The Way It Is*
'Unchained Melody' (North & Zaret)	1977	LP *Moody Blue*
'Until It's Time For You To Go' (Sante-Marie)	1971	single; LP *Elvis Now*
'Up Above My Head' (Brown)	1968	LP *Elvis – TV Special*
'US Male' (Hubbard)	1968	single; LP *Almost In Love*
'Vino, Dinero Y Amor' (Tepper & Bennett)	1963	LP *Fun In Acapulco*
'Viva Las Vegas!' (Pomus & Schuman)	1963	single; LP *Worldwide 50 Gold Award Hits 1*
'Walls Have Ears' (Tepper & Bennett)	1962	LP *Girls! Girls! Girls!*
'Walk A Mile In My Shoes' (South)	1970	LP *February 1970 – On Stage*
'Way Down' (Martine Jnr.)	1976	LP *Moody Blue*
'Wear My Ring Around Your Neck' (Carroll & Moody)	1958	single; LP *Elvis' Golden Records 2*
'Wearin' That Loved On Look' (Frazier & Owens)	1969	LP *From Elvis In Memphis*
'We Call On Him' (Karger, Weisman & Wayne)	1967	single; LP *You'll Never Walk Alone*
'We Can Make The Morning' (Ramsey)	1971	single; LP *Elvis Now*
'Welcome To My World' (Winkler & Hathcock)	1973	LP *Aloha From Hawaii*
'We'll Be Together' (O'Curran & Brooks)	1962	LP *Girls! Girls! Girls!*
'We're Coming In Loaded' (Blackwell & Scott)	1962	LP *Girls! Girls! Girls!*
'We're Gonna Move' (Matson & Presley)	1956	LP *A Date With Elvis*
'Western Union' (Tepper & Bennett)	1963	LP *Speedway*
'What A Wonderful Life' (Wayne & Livingstone)	1961	LP *I Got Lucky*
'What'd I Say?' (Charles)	1963	single; LP *Elvis' Golden Records 4*
'What Every Woman Lives For' (Pomus & Schuman)	1965	LP *Frankie & Johnny*
'What Now, My Love' (Sigman & Becaud)	1973	LP *Aloha From Hawaii*
'What Now, What Next, Where To?' (Robinson & Blair)	1963	LP *Double Trouble*
'What's She Really Like?' (Wayne & Silver)	1960	LP *G.I. Blues*
'Wheels On My Heels' (Tepper & Bennett)	1964	LP *Roustabout*
'When I'm Over You' (Milete)	1970	LP *Love Letters From Elvis*
'When It Rains It Really Pours' (Emerson)	1957	LP *Elvis For Everyone*
'When My Blue Moon Turns To Gold Again' (Walker & Sullivan)	1956	LP *Elvis*
'When The Saints Go Marching In' (Trad. arranged Presley)	1965	LP *Frankie & Johnny*

126

'Where Could I Go To But To The Lord' (Coats)	1966	LP *How Great Thou Art*
'Where Did They Go, Lord?' (Frazier & Owens)	1970	single
'Where Do I Go From Here?' (Williams)	1972	LP *Elvis*
'Where Do You Come From?' (Batchelor & Roberts)	1962	single; LP *Girls! Girls! Girls!*
'Where No One Stands Alone' (Lister)	1966	LP *How Great Thou Art*
'White Christmas' (Berlin)	1957	LP *Elvis' Christmas Album*
'Who Am I?' (Goodman)	1969	LP *You'll Never Walk Alone*
'Who Are You?' (Wayne & Weisman)	1967	LP *Speedway*
'Whole Lotta Shakin' Goin' On' (Williams & David)	1970	LP *Elvis Country*
'Who Needs Money?' (Starr)	1967	LP *Clambake*
'Why Me, Lord?' (Kristofferson)	1974	LP *Elvis Live In Memphis*
'Wild In The Country' (Peretti, Creatore & Weiss)	1960	single; LP *Worldwide Gold Award Hits 2*
'Winter Wonderland' (Smith & Bernard)	1971	LP *Elvis Sings The Wonderful World of Christmas*
'Wisdom Of The Ages' (Giant, Baum & Kaye)	1965	LP *Harum Scarum*
'Witchcraft' (Bartholomew & King)	1963	single; LP *Elvis' Golden Records 4*
'Without Him' (Lefevre)	1966	LP *How Great Thou Art*
'Without Love (There Is Nothing)' (Small)	1969	LP *Back In Memphis*
'Wolf Call' (Giant, Baum & Kaye)	1964	LP *Girl Happy*
'Woman Without Love' (Chesnut)	1975	LP *Today*
'Wonderful World' (Fletcher & Flett)	1968	LP *Elvis Sings Flaming Star*
'Wonderful World of Christmas' (Tobias & Frisch)	1971	LP *Elvis Sings The Wonderful World of Christmas*
'Wonder Of You' (Baker & Knights)	1970	single; LP *Worldwide Gold Award Hits 2*
'Wonders You Perform' (Trad. arranged Presley)	1973	LP *From Elvis Presley Boulevard*
'Wooden Heart' (Weis, Weisman & Twomey)	1960	single; LP *G.I. Blues*
'Words' (Gibb Brothers)	1969	LP *From Memphis To Vegas*
'Working On The Building' (Hoyle & Bowles)	1960	LP *His Hand In Mine*
'Yellow Rose Of Texas' (Wise & Starr)	1963	LP *Elvis Sings Flaming Star*
'Yesterday' (Lennon & McCartney)	1969	LP *February 1970 – On Stage*
'Yoga Is As Yoga Does' (Nelson & Burch)	1966	LP *I Got Lucky*
'You Asked Me To' (Jennings & Shaver)	1973	LP *Promised Land*
'You Can't Say No In Acapulco' (Feller, Morris & Fuller)	1963	LP *Fun In Acapulco*
'You Don't Have To Say You Love Me' (Wickham, Napier-Bell, Donnaggio & Pallavicini)	1970	single; LP *Elvis – That's The Way It Is*
'You Don't Know Me' (Walker & Arnold)	1967	single; LP *Clambake*
'You Gave Me A Mountain' (Robbins)	1972	LP *Aloha From Hawaii*
'You Gotta Stop' (Giant, Baum & Kaye)	1966	LP *I Got Lucky*
'You'll Be Gone' (West, Hodge & Presley)	1962	single; LP *Girl Happy*
'You'll Never Walk Alone' (Rodgers & Hammerstein)	1967	single; LP *You'll Never Walk Alone*
'You'll Think Of Me' (Schuman)	1969	single; LP *From Memphis To Vegas*
'Young And Beautiful' (Silver & Schroeder)	1957	single; LP *A Date With Elvis*
'Young Dreams' (Kalmanoff & Schroeder)	1958	LP *King Creole*
'Your Cheatin' Heart' (Williams)	1958	LP *Elvis For Everyone*
'You're A Heartbreaker' (Sallee)	1954	single; LP *The Sun Sessions*
'Your Love's Been A Long Time Coming' (Bourke)	1973	LP *Promised Land*
'Your Time Hasn't Come Yet, Baby' (Hirschorn & Kasna)	1967	single; LP *Speedway*
'You've Lost That Lovin' Feelin'' (Mann & Weil)	1970	LP *Elvis – That's The Way It Is*

The King of entertainers – 'And I Love You So' (1977).